THE
SIMPLE SUBSTITUTIONS
COOKBOOK

ADAPTING RECIPES TO YOUR TASTE

Sandra Rudloff

Bristol Publishing Enterprises
Hayward, California

A nitty gritty® Cookbook

©2004 Bristol Publishing Enterprises, Inc., 2714 McCone Ave., Hayward, CA 94545. World rights reserved.
No part of this publication may be reproduced in any form, nor may it be stored in a retrieval system, transmitted,
or otherwise copied for public or private use without prior written permission from the publisher.
Printed in the United States of America.
ISBN: 1-55867-291-5
Adapted from *Flexible Fare,* ISBN: 1-55867-228-1

Cover design: Frank J. Paredes
Cover photography: John A. Benson
Food stylist: Susan Devaty
Illustrator: Shanti Nelson

CONTENTS

ACKNOWLEDGMENTS

Thanks go to Chris, Jonathan and Stephen Rudloff for their love, patience and their support while I worked on this book; to my mother and late father, Betty and Sylvester Fanucchi, for giving me my love of cooking; to Evonne Fawley for the inspiration and ideas; to everyone at Space Designs, Inc., for their willingness to taste test; and to Jennifer Newens for taking a chance.

DON'T BE A RECIPE SLAVE!

Have you ever seen someone in a supermarket with a copy of a recipe in hand, shopping for the ingredients? Or has someone ever prepared you a meal that you didn't quite like because of one or two ingredients? Are you a "recipe slave?" If your answer to any of these questions is, "Yes" then you will find this book useful.

One of the first concepts taught at most cooking schools is that a recipe is a template. The ingredients were chosen by the chef to his or her specifications. And of course, not everyone likes the same foods. A great recipe to one may not be to another, simply because of a single ingredient.

The Simple Substitutions Cookbook shows how a recipe can be varied to suit different tastes and available ingredients. Almost all recipes have at least two variations, including an addition, a substitution or an ingredient omitted. By changing one or two items in a recipe, you can create your own signature dishes. But don't be limited by the variations listed. Once you see how easily variations can be made, you can add, change or omit other ingredients to your taste.

There are some ingredients that you should not change, like yeast, baking powder and baking soda, which are critical to the texture of baked goods.

SUBSTITUTION TIPS TABLE

The first step to modifying recipes is look for easy substitutions, eliminating one ingredient and using a similar ingredient, using the same quantity and in the same manner. A beginning substitution table is provided to help you understand and give you insight on how to manipulate recipes.

Instead of	Try an equal amount of
apples	pears
artichoke hearts	asparagus
beef or chicken broth	water or vegetable broth
blackberries	raspberries or strawberries
brandy	sherry
broccoli	cauliflower
cantaloupe	honeydew melon
cheddar cheese	Swiss cheese
chicken	turkey
chicken breasts	pork tenderloin
chives	green onions
cider vinegar	white vinegar
cinnamon	cardamom, allspice or nutmeg
couscous	tiny pasta (pastina or orzo)
cream	half-and-half
crookneck squash	zucchini
dried apricots	dried pears or dried apples
dried basil	dried oregano

fettuccine	spaghetti
ground beef	ground turkey
ketchup	mild chili sauce
kidney beans	black beans
lemon juice	lime juice
milk chocolate	bittersweet chocolate
mozzarella cheese	provolone cheese
orange juice	grapefruit juice
peaches	pears
pepperoni	salami
pork	chicken breast
raisins	currants or dried cranberries
red potatoes	white potatoes
salmon	swordfish or shark
shrimp	crabmeat
snow pea pods	sugar snap peas
spinach (cooked)	Swiss chard (cooked)
turnips	parsnips
veal	chicken
walnuts	almonds or pecans
white rice	brown rice or wild rice
yams	sweet potatoes
yellow onions	white or red onions

OMITTING AND ADDING INGREDIENTS

Some ingredients in your recipes should not be omitted or changed, like leavening agents. In reviewing a recipe, it is important to visualize how your omission or addition could change the recipe. Omitting a single ingredient, if it is central to the recipe, can radically change the taste or texture of a recipe. Adding an ingredient will also change the taste and texture, but could also change the quantity of a dish (adding a spice or seasoning would not add much volume, but adding a cup of nuts or an additional vegetable would increase the amount of a dish). When adding or omitting ingredients, it is important to remember that the other ingredients will become more or less prominent.

The variations listed with each recipe show both additions and omissions to the basic recipe. These changes should give an idea of the types of adjustments that can easily be made. Most of the time, you can combine some of the alternate recipes to create another variation of the basic recipe.

It is vital to recognize each ingredient in a recipe as a separate item. The next time you are at a restaurant, try to distinguish the individual tastes of the item you ordered. You may be surprised how easy it will be to re-create restaurant dishes at home once you master this technique.

BREADS AND BREAKFASTS

APPLE CURRANT SCONES

Makes 12–16 scones

These scones have a rustic appearance because they are dropped, rather than rolled out.

¼ cup apple juice
½ cup dried currants
½ cup finely chopped dried apples
1 cup buttermilk
¼ cup (½ stick) butter, melted and cooled

¼ cup sugar
2 cups flour
1 tbs. baking powder
1 tsp. baking soda

Heat oven to 350°. In a small saucepan, bring apple juice to a boil. Stir in currants and apples. Remove from heat, cover pan and let stand for 15 minutes. In a large bowl, beat together buttermilk, butter and sugar. Stir in currant-apple mixture and any unabsorbed apple juice. Add flour, baking powder and baking soda, mixing just until incorporated. Drop batter by ¼-cupfuls onto a cookie sheet. Bake for 14 to 17 minutes, until tops are golden. Transfer scones to a wire rack to cool. Store in an airtight container.

APPLE CURRANT SCONES WITH WALNUTS

Add ½ cup chopped walnuts to buttermilk batter.

APPLE CRANBERRY OR APRICOT SCONES

Substitute ½ cup dried cranberries or chopped dried apricots for the currants.

CLASSIC BUTTERMILK BISCUITS

A good buttermilk biscuit recipe can be the base for dozens of other variations. Create your own signature biscuits by adding chopped nuts or fresh herbs from your garden.

2 cups flour
2 tsp. baking powder
1/4 tsp. baking soda

1 tsp. salt
1/4 cup vegetable shortening
3/4 cup buttermilk

Heat oven to 450°. In a large bowl, mix flour, baking powder, baking soda and salt. With a pastry blender or 2 knives, cut shortening into flour mixture until the mixture resembles coarse crumbs. Add buttermilk and stir with a fork until just mixed, and dough is soft. Transfer dough to a lightly floured work surface and knead 6 or 8 times. Roll out dough to about 1/2-inch thick. With a 2-inch biscuit cutter, cut biscuits into rounds. Place biscuits on an ungreased cookie sheet. Bake for 12 to 15 minutes, until golden,.

SUNFLOWER OR POPPYSEED BUTTERMILK BISCUITS

Before adding buttermilk, add 1/4 cup roasted, shelled sunflower seeds or 2 tbs. poppyseeds.

BUTTERMILK BISCUITS WITH CHIVES

Before adding buttermilk, add 1/4 cup minced fresh chives.

CINNAMON-PECAN ROLLS

Serve warm cinnamon-pecan rolls with piping hot coffee for your next Sunday brunch.

½ cup granulated sugar

½ tsp. salt

3½ tsp. active dry yeast

4½–5 cups flour, divided

¾ cup (1½ sticks) butter, melted, divided

1 cup warm milk (110°)

2 eggs

½ cup brown sugar, packed

1 cup chopped pecans

1½ tsp. cinnamon

2 cups confectioners' sugar

¾ tsp. vanilla extract

3 tbs. water

Spray a 9 x 13-inch baking pan with nonstick spray. Combine granulated sugar, salt, yeast and 2 cups of the flour in a large bowl; set aside. In a small bowl combine ½ cup of the butter with milk. With a mixer on low speed, gradually beat milk and butter into the flour mixture. Add eggs, increase speed to medium, and beat for 2 minutes. With a spoon, stir in 2 to 2½ cups of the remaining flour to make a soft dough (you may not need to use all of the flour.) Transfer dough to a lightly floured work surface and knead with the heels of your hands about 10 minutes until smooth and elastic. Shape dough into a ball and place in a large oiled bowl, turning dough to coat all sides with oil. Cover bowl lightly with a towel and set in a warm place to rise until doubled in size, about 1 hour.

Punch down dough. Cover and let rest for 15 minutes while you prepare the filling. Combine brown sugar, pecans and cinnamon in a small bowl. Set aside. On a lightly floured work surface, roll dough into a 18-x-12-inch rectangle. Brush dough with melted butter and sprinkle evenly with filling. Starting at the 18-inch side, roll dough jelly roll-style. Pinch seams to seal. Slice the dough into 15 slices. Place rolls in prepared pan, cut side down. Cover rolls loosely with a towel and set in a warm place to rise until doubled, about 40 minutes. Heat oven to 350°.

Bake rolls for 20 to 25 minutes, until lightly browned. Cool in pan for 10 minutes. In a small bowl, beat confectioners' sugar, vanilla, and water until smooth, and drizzle over rolls. Serve warm.

HONEY CINNAMON PECAN ROLLS
Substitute ½ cup honey for the sugar in the yeast dough.

PECAN ROLLS
Omit cinnamon.

CINNAMON WALNUT ROLLS
Substitute walnuts for the pecans.

CINNAMON RAISIN PECAN ROLLS
Add ½ cup raisins to filling mixture.

CHEDDAR CHEESE MUFFINS

Try adding crumbled bacon or minced ham to personalize these savory muffins.

2 tbs. butter

¼ cup minced fresh chives

2 cups flour

2 tsp. baking powder

¾ tsp. salt

2 tbs. sugar

2 eggs

1 cup milk

1 cup shredded sharp yellow cheddar cheese

Heat oven to 350°. Spray a muffin pan with nonstick spray. Over medium heat, melt butter in a small skillet. Add chives and remove from heat; set aside. In a small bowl, stir together flour, baking powder, salt and sugar. Set aside. In a medium bowl, beat together eggs and milk. Beat in chive mixture and cheddar. Add flour mixture, stirring only enough to blend thoroughly. Spoon mixture into prepared muffin cups, filling each about ⅔ full. Bake for 20 to 25 minutes, or until muffin tops just begin to brown. Remove muffins from cups. Cool on a wire rack.

WHITE CHEDDAR CHEESE MUFFINS

Substitute 1 cup shredded white cheddar cheese for the yellow cheddar cheese.

CHEDDAR CHEESE AND SHALLOT MUFFINS

Substitute 1 minced shallot for the chives.

HERB CHEESE BREAD

For an easy appetizer, cut this into thin slices and serve with cheese at your next dinner party.

2¼ cups flour
2 tsp. baking powder
1 tsp. salt
½ tsp. baking soda
2 eggs
3 tbs. butter, melted and cooled

1¼ cups buttermilk
1 cup shredded Monterey Jack cheese
¼ cup chopped fresh parsley
2 tbs. chopped fresh chives
1 tsp. dried basil
1 tsp. sugar

Heat oven to 350°. Spray two 9 x 5-inch loaf pans with nonstick spray. In a small bowl, blend flour, baking powder, salt and baking soda. In a large bowl, beat eggs; beat in butter and buttermilk. Stir in cheese, parsley, chives, basil and sugar. Add flour mixture, mixing only enough to moisten. Fill prepared pans with batter. Bake for 50 minutes, or until a toothpick inserted in the center comes out clean. Cool in pans for 5 minutes, then turn loaves out onto a wire rack to cool.

CHEDDAR HERB BREAD
Substitute shredded sharp cheddar cheese for the Monterey Jack.

SUN-DRIED TOMATO AND CHEESE BREAD
Substitute ¼ cup minced sun-dried tomatoes for the parsley and basil.

CARROT RAISIN SPICE BREAD

This makes a great breakfast bread or lunch box treat. Try it spread with cream cheese, or toasted and buttered. The carrots, zucchini and raisins makes this bread a healthy indulgence. Add chopped nuts for crunch.

1/3 cup sugar
1/3 cup vegetable shortening
2 eggs
3/4 cup shredded zucchini
3/4 cup shredded carrots
1/3 cup apple juice
1 tsp. vanilla extract
1 2/3 cups flour

1/2 tsp. cinnamon
1/2 tsp. ground cloves
1/2 tsp. ground allspice
1 tsp. baking soda
1/4 tsp. baking powder
3/4 tsp. salt
2/3 cup raisins

Heat oven to 350°. Prepare a 9 x 5-inch loaf pan by greasing and flouring bottom and sides. In a large bowl, beat sugar and shortening with a mixer until light and fluffy. Add eggs and beat well. Fold in zucchini, carrots, apple juice and vanilla. In a small bowl, combine flour, cinnamon, cloves, allspice, baking soda, baking powder and salt; add to carrot mixture. Add raisins, mixing to incorporate only.

Pour batter into prepared pan. Bake for 1 hour, or until a toothpick inserted into the center comes out clean. Cool in pan for 5 minutes, then transfer bread to a cooling rack; cool completely. Store tightly wrapped in the refrigerator.

ZUCCHINI RAISIN SPICE BREAD

Omit carrots. Increase amount of shredded zucchini to 1½ cups.

CARROT NUT SPICE BREAD

Substitute ⅔ cup chopped walnuts or pecans for the raisins.

JALAPEÑO CORNBREAD

This bread has a bit of fire to it, so keep a cold drink within reach!

1 cup yellow cornmeal
1 cup flour
2 tbs. sugar
1 tbs. baking powder
1 tsp. salt
1/2 tsp. baking soda

3/4 cup buttermilk
3 eggs
1/4 cup (1/2 stick) butter, melted and cooled
1 cup shredded sharp cheddar cheese
1 can (4 oz.) diced jalapeño peppers, drained

Heat oven to 450°. Spray an 8-inch square baking pan with nonstick cooking spray. In a large bowl, blend cornmeal, flour, sugar, baking powder, salt and baking soda. In a small bowl, mix together buttermilk, eggs, butter, cheese and jalapeños. Pour buttermilk mixture into cornmeal-flour mixture and stir only until combined. Pour batter into prepared pan. Bake for 20 minutes. Cool cornbread in pan for 5 minutes before serving.

GREEN CHILE CORNBREAD

Substitute 1 can (4 oz.) mild green chiles, drained, for the jalapeños.

BACON AND JALAPEÑO CORNBREAD

Add 1/2 cup cooked crumbled bacon when adding the jalapeños.

OATMEAL HONEY BREAD

This bread's especially good topped with jam and butter. Save the leftovers for French toast.

1 cup warm water (110°), divided
1 pkg. active dry yeast
1/4 cup honey
2 tsp. butter, melted

1 tsp. salt
1/2 cup quick-cooking oats
2 1/2–2 3/4 cups bread flour, divided

Pour 1/4 cup of the warm water into a large bowl. Stir in yeast and let stand for 5 minutes. Add remaining 3/4 cup water, honey, butter, salt, oats and 1 cup of the bread flour. With a mixer at low speed, beat ingredients until just mixed. Increase speed to medium and add 1/2 cup of the flour to make a thick batter. Stir in enough additional flour by hand to make a stiff dough. Cover bowl with a towel and set in a warm place to rise about 1 hour until doubled in size. Punch dough down. Grease bottom and sides of a 2-quart round casserole. Shape dough into a ball and place in prepared dish. Cover with a towel and let rise 30 to 45 minutes until doubled in size.

Heat oven to 350°. Bake for about 40 minutes or until the bread sounds hollow when tapped. Remove bread from oven and immediately remove from dish to a wire rack to cool.

OATMEAL MAPLE BREAD

Substitute pure maple syrup for the honey.

EGG BREAD

Egg bread turns French toast into a morning treat. The golden color and gentle flavor make this a good bread for any occasion. And it can handle any number of additions, from herbs or sun-dried tomatoes to dried cranberries or apricots.

1 pkg. active dry yeast
1/4 cup warm water (110°)
1 cup warm milk (110°)
3 eggs
1/2 cup vegetable oil
2 tsp. salt
1/4 cup sugar
5 1/2 cups bread flour

In a large bowl, dissolve yeast in warm water. In another bowl, beat together milk, eggs and oil. Stir into yeast. Add salt, sugar and flour, stirring to make a soft dough. Turn dough out onto a lightly floured surface and knead about 5 minutes until smooth and elastic. Lightly oil a large bowl. Place dough in bowl and turn to coat dough all sides with oil. Cover and let rise in a warm place about 1 hour until doubled in size.

Punch dough down. Place dough on a work surface and let rest for 10 minutes. Cut dough in half and shape each half into a loaf. Spray two 9 x 5-inch loaf pans with cooking spray. Place each loaf into a pan. Cover loaves and let rise about 45 minutes until doubled in size. Heat oven to 350°. Bake loaves about 40 minutes until the tops are brown and loaves sound hollow when tapped. Cool in pan for 5 minutes; turn loaves out onto a cooling rack.

RAISIN EGG BREAD

Knead 2 cups raisins into dough before the first rise.

HONEY EGG BREAD

Substitute ¼ cup honey for the sugar.

ROSEMARY AND GARLIC FOCACCIA

This bread makes great sandwiches; try it with prosciutto, provolone and tomato. In yeast breads, use raw garlic only for a topping as it might retard yeast growth.

1 pkg. active dry yeast
1/4 cup warm water (110°)
1 1/4 cups warm milk (110°)
1/2 cup olive oil, divided
3–3 1/2 cups bread flour, divided
1 cup fine semolina flour
1 tsp. salt
1 tbs. minced fresh rosemary
3 cloves garlic, minced

In a large bowl, stir yeast into water and let stand for 5 minutes. Add milk, 6 tbs. of the olive oil, 3 cups of the bread flour, semolina flour and salt. Stir to make a soft dough. Transfer dough to a floured surface and knead until smooth and elastic, adding more flour if needed. Place dough in a large oiled bowl and turn to coat all sides with oil. Cover with a towel and set in a warm place about 1 1/2 hours until doubled in size.

Punch down dough and transfer to a lightly floured work surface. Sprinkle rosemary over dough and knead in lightly. Oil a 15 x 10-inch jelly roll pan. With your hands, gently spread dough to fit pan and cover dough with a towel. Let dough rise about 30 minutes until doubled in size. Heat oven to 350°. With your fingers, lightly dimple dough and brush with remaining 2 tbs. olive oil. Sprinkle with garlic. Bake focaccia for 20 to 25 minutes until lightly golden brown on top. Cool for 20 minutes before cutting.

PINE NUT AND PARMESAN FOCACCIA

Substitute ½ cup shredded Parmesan cheese and ½ cup pine nuts for the rosemary. Omit garlic. Knead into the dough before the second rise.

SUN-DRIED TOMATO AND GARLIC FOCACCIA

Substitute ¼ cup minced sun-dried tomatoes for rosemary. Knead into the dough before the second rise.

RUSTIC BREAD

Makes 2 loaves

This soft, chewy bread is great for hearty sandwiches, or for dipping into Olive Oil Dipping Sauce, *page 27. If the bread gets stale, cut it into cubes, toast with a little olive oil, and you've got crunchy croutons.*

1 pkg. active dry yeast
2 cups warm water (110°)
1 tsp. sugar
1 tsp. salt
5 cups bread flour

In a large bowl, stir yeast into ½ cup of the water and let stand for 5 minutes. Add remaining 1½ cups water, sugar, salt and flour. With a mixer on low speed or by hand, beat until flour is thoroughly incorporated. (Dough will be sticky, not smooth.) Place dough in a large oiled bowl and turn to coat all sides with oil. Cover with a towel and set in a warm place to rise for about 1½ hours until doubled in size.

Punch dough down and transfer to a lightly floured work surface. Knead briefly to eliminate air bubbles. Cut dough in half. With floured hands, shape each piece into a 12-inch log. Place logs on a cookie sheet a few inches apart and cover with a towel. Let rise for 30 minutes. Heat oven to 400°. Bake bread for about 40 minutes, until it sounds hollow when tapped. Cool completely on a rack before cutting.

RUSTIC BREAD WITH OLIVES

Add 1 cup coarsely chopped kalamata or other brine-cured olives as you knead out the air bubbles. Knead only enough to incorporate olives.

RUSTIC BREAD WITH WALNUTS

Add 1 cup chopped walnuts as you knead out the air bubbles. Knead only enough to incorporate nuts.

POTATO AND SAUSAGE FRITTATA

Frittatas are perfect for brunches and light suppers and go nicely with a tossed green salad. You can also bake the frittata in a skillet with an ovenproof handle.

6 oz. bulk pork breakfast sausage
1 tbs. olive oil
1½ cups cubed red-skinned potato (about 1
   large potato)

2 medium zucchini, cut into ½-inch cubes
8 eggs
¼ cup shredded Parmesan cheese
¼ tsp. pepper

Heat oven to 350°. Spray an 8 x 8-inch baking pan with nonstick cooking spray.

In a medium skillet over medium-high heat, crumble sausage. Sauté until cooked through but not brown. Remove from skillet and drain on paper towels. Discard any fat. Add olive oil to skillet. Add potato and cook about 10 minutes until potato just begins to brown. Remove potato from skillet and set aside. Add zucchini to skillet and sauté about 5 minutes until it just begins to soften. Remove from heat. Spread potatoes evenly on the bottom of prepared baking pan. Place sausage evenly over potatoes. Top sausage with zucchini.

In a medium bowl, combine eggs, Parmesan and pepper. Mix well and pour over vegetable-meat mixture in baking pan. Bake frittata for 20 to 25 minutes or just until center is set. Serve immediately.

POTATO AND ZUCCHINI FRITTATA
 Omit sausage.

POTATO, SAUSAGE AND ONION FRITTATA
 Substitute 1 chopped yellow onion, sautéed in olive oil until translucent, for the zucchini. Layer cooked onions on top of sausage.

SUMMER FRITTATA

Use any vegetable ready for harvest from your garden and add your favorite fresh herbs.

2 tbs. olive oil
1 yellow onion, chopped
6 medium zucchini, chopped
4 large tomatoes, chopped and drained

8 eggs
1/3 cup shredded Parmesan cheese
1/4 tsp. pepper

Heat oven to 350°. Spray a 9 x 13-inch baking pan with nonstick cooking spray. In a large skillet, heat oil over medium-high heat. Add onion and sauté about 8 minutes until onion begins to brown. Add zucchini and cook for 4 minutes. Cool to room temperature. Add tomatoes and stir gently.

In a large bowl, beat eggs well. Add Parmesan and pepper and mix until thoroughly combined. Gently fold in tomato-zucchini mixture. Pour mixture into prepared dish. Bake for 45 to 60 minutes or until firm in center. Serve immediately or cool and serve at room temperature.

ARTICHOKE FRITTATA

Substitute 3 cups chopped artichoke hearts for the zucchini.

SUMMER FRITTATA WITH RICOTTA

Add 1 lb. ricotta cheese to beaten eggs before adding the vegetables

SOUR CREAM QUICHE

Servings: 6-8

This quiche is a bit firmer than regular cream quiches. It holds up well to the addition of vegetables, meats or other variations.

4 eggs
2 cups sour cream
10 slices bacon, cooked and crumbled
½ tsp. salt

¼ tsp. ground nutmeg
1¼ cups shredded Swiss cheese
one 9-inch, deep-dish unbaked piecrust

Heat oven to 425°. In a large bowl, beat together eggs and sour cream. Mix in bacon, salt, nutmeg and cheese. Pour egg mixture into piecrust. Bake for 15 minutes. Reduce oven heat to 350° and bake for an additional 45 minutes, until golden brown. Let stand at room temperature for 10 minutes before serving.

MEXICAN QUICHE

Substitute pepper Jack cheese for the Swiss cheese. Omit bacon and nutmeg and add 1 can (4 oz.) chopped mild green chiles, drained.

BROCCOLI OR SPINACH QUICHE

Add 1 cup chopped cooked broccoli or spinach, drained. Omit nutmeg.

APPETIZERS

OLIVE OIL DIPPING SAUCE

Use one of these dippers as a substitute for butter at your next meal. Not only is olive oil more flavorful, but it is also more healthful.

1 cup extra-virgin olive oil
1 tsp. dried oregano
1 clove garlic, minced

¼ tsp. pepper
2 tbs. balsamic vinegar

In a small container, combine all ingredients. Let flavors blend for a minimum of 3 hours. Mix well and pour on a shallow plate.

BASIL OLIVE OIL DIPPING SAUCE
Substitute dried basil for the oregano.

GARLIC OLIVE OIL DIPPING SAUCE
Use 2 cloves garlic instead of just 1.

FIERY OLIVE OIL DIPPING SAUCE
Add ¼ tsp. crushed red peppers flakes.

MIXED HERB OLIVE OIL DIPPING SAUCE
Add 1 tbs. minced fresh chives.

RED WINE AND OLIVE OIL DIPPING SAUCE
Substitute 1 tbs. red wine vinegar for the balsamic vinegar.

MOZZARELLA CHEESE BITES

These herbed cheese treats are perfect with wine, thinly sliced French baguettes, seedless red or green grapes and other cheeses for your next gathering.

2 tbs. minced fresh chives
2 tbs. minced fresh Italian parsley
2 cloves garlic, minced
$1/4$ cup olive oil
2 tbs. apple cider vinegar

$1/4$ tsp. salt
$1/4$ tsp. pepper
8 oz. mozzarella cheese, cut into 1-inch cubes
sliced French baguette for serving

In a medium bowl, combine chives, parsley, garlic, olive oil, vinegar, salt and pepper and stir to combine. Add mozzarella and stir to mix. Cover and refrigerate for at least 3 hours. Place on a serving dish and serve with sliced baguettes.

BASIL MOZZARELLA CHEESE BITES
Substitute 2 tbs. minced fresh basil for the parsley.

PROVENCE HERBED CHEESE BITES
Substitute 2 tbs. minced fresh chervil for the parsley.

PESTO PALMIERS

'Palmiers' or 'palm leaves' are made from puff pastry dough, folded, rolled, cut into strips and baked. These appetizers are so addictive. You can assemble them early in the day and pop them into the oven when guests arrive.

2 sheets frozen puff pastry, thawed $2/3$ cup prepared basil pesto, divided

Spray a cookie sheet with nonstick cooking spray. Lay one pastry sheet flat on a work surface. Spread $1/3$ cup of the pesto evenly over pastry. Starting from one short side, roll up jelly roll-style to center. Starting at the second short side, roll up to the center. Press two sides together and wrap in plastic wrap. Place in refrigerator to chill for 1 hour. Repeat with second pastry sheet and remaining pesto. Heat oven to 400°. Remove pastry from plastic wrap. Slice $1/2$-inch thick and arrange on prepared cookie sheet, cut-side down and spaced 1 inch apart. Bake for about 20 minutes or until golden brown. Serve warm.

SUN-DRIED TOMATO PESTO PALMIERS
Substitute sun-dried tomato pesto for the basil pesto.

PARMESAN PALMIERS
Substitute $1/2$ cup shredded Parmesan cheese for the basil pesto.

OLIVADA SPREAD

Usually served with sliced baguettes, this spread can also be rubbed on chicken before roasting for a Tuscan-style chicken dinner.

1 tsp. olive oil
1 anchovy fillet
1 clove garlic
1 cup pitted kalamata olives

In a blender container or food processor workbowl, combine olive oil, anchovy and garlic. Pulse until mixture becomes a smooth paste. Add olives and pulse until mixture is well chopped, but not smooth. Place olivada into a small container, cover and refrigerate for at least 4 hours to blend flavors. Serve with baguette slices.

GREEN OLIVADA SPREAD

Substitute 1 cup green pimiento-stuffed olives for the kalamata olives.

ROSEMARY OLIVADA SPREAD

Add 1 tsp. fresh chopped rosemary.

SPINACH-STUFFED PORTOBELLO MUSHROOMS

Servings: 4

Large, meaty portobellos are a creative change from the standard stuffed mushroom caps.

1 pkg. (10 oz.) frozen chopped spinach,
    thawed and squeezed dry
2 eggs
1/3 cup minced yellow onion
1 clove garlic, minced
1/4 tsp. salt

1/4 cup grated Parmesan cheese
1/4 tsp. ground nutmeg
1/2 cup fresh breadcrumbs
2 portobello mushrooms, 4–5 inches in
    diameter

Heat oven to 450°. In a large bowl, combine spinach, eggs, onion, garlic, salt, Parmesan, nutmeg and breadcrumbs. Stir to mix thoroughly. Remove stems from mushrooms; rinse and dry caps. Gently mound 1/2 of the spinach mixture on the gill side of each mushroom cap. Place mushrooms on an ungreased cookie sheet and bake for 20 to 25 minutes. Cool for a few minutes. Cut into wedges and serve.

SAUSAGE-STUFFED PORTOBELLO MUSHROOMS
Use only 1/2 pkg. spinach and add 1/3 cup cooked, crumbled Italian sausage to filling.

CHEESE-STUFFED PORTOBELLO MUSHROOMS
Substitute 1 cup ricotta cheese for the spinach. Increase Parmesan to 1/2 cup.

PORK PILLOWS

The shape of these Asian-style dumplings resembles small pillows. Their handy size will work well as an appetizer at your next dinner party.

1 lb. ground pork
1 egg
1 clove garlic, minced
1 tbs. soy sauce
2 tsp. ground ginger
1/4 tsp. salt
1/2 tsp. sesame oil

1/4 cup chopped fresh cilantro
3 tbs. chopped green onions
2 tbs. cornstarch
2 tbs. water
1 pkg. 2-inch square won ton wrappers
vegetable shortening for deep-frying

In a medium skillet, crumble ground pork and sauté over medium-high heat until cooked through, about 10 minutes. Drain fat and set pork aside. In a medium bowl, beat together egg, garlic, soy sauce, ginger, salt and sesame oil. Mix in pork, cilantro and green onions.

To assemble pillows, dissolve cornstarch in water in a small bowl. Place a won ton wrapper on a work surface and brush edges with cornstarch mixture. Place 1 heaping tbs. of the pork mixture onto center of wrapper. Top meat mixture with another won ton wrapper and press edges together to seal well. Repeat with remaining filling and won ton wrappers.

Melt shortening in a wok or a deep saucepan over medium-high heat to about 2 inches deep. Place a few pillows in hot shortening, being careful not to overcrowd or have pillows touch each other. Deep-fry until golden brown, 3 to 5 minutes. Remove with a slotted spoon and drain on paper towels. Repeat with remaining pillows. Serve hot.

PORK SPRING PILLOWS
Add 1/2 cup shredded carrots and 1/2 cup shredded cabbage to filling.

SHRIMP PILLOWS
Substitute 1 lb. cooked chopped shrimp for the cooked pork.

SAUSAGE POLENTA SQUARES

When cooked polenta cools it becomes very firm and can be sliced. The slices are solid enough to stand up to a heavy topping and make perfect appetizers. Try this polenta as a side dish instead of pasta or rice.

½ lb. bulk Italian sausage	¼ tsp. dried basil
½ yellow onion, minced	¼ tsp. salt
1 can (8 oz.) tomato sauce	1 tsp. sugar
½ cup red wine or beef broth	*Polenta,* page 75
¼ tsp. dried oregano	olive oil

Crumble sausage into a large skillet. Sauté sausage over high heat until it begins to brown; drain fat. Add onion, reduce heat to medium and sauté until onion is translucent. Add tomato sauce, wine, oregano, basil, salt and sugar and bring mixture to a boil. Reduce heat to low and simmer uncovered for 25 to 30 minutes or until thickened. Keep warm.

Heat broiler. Slice cooked polenta into ½-inch-thick slices, about 2 inches square. Place polenta squares on a very lightly oiled cookie sheet and brush tops with a small amount of olive oil. Broil for 5 to 8 minutes per side or until lightly browned. Place on paper towels to drain.

Place 1 tbs. of the sausage mixture on each polenta square and serve immediately.

CHEESE AND PROSCIUTTO POLENTA SQUARES

Omit sauce. Top each broiled polenta square with a slice of prosciutto (about 4 oz. total) and about 1 tbs. shredded mozzarella cheese (about 1 cup total). Broil polenta squares for an additional 3 to 5 minutes or until cheese is melted. Serve immediately.

SWEET RED PEPPER POLENTA SQUARES

Omit sausage. Add 2 tbs. butter to skillet and sauté 1 cup chopped red bell peppers with the onion. Proceed with recipe.

GRILLED QUESADILLAS WITH SALSA CRUDA

Servings: 4

This is a great appetizer to nibble on while you are at the grill. Try using some of the flavored tortillas that are now on the market, such as spinach, tomato or chile.

2 cups chopped tomatoes
1/4 cup minced red onion
1/4 cup chopped fresh cilantro
1/4 tsp. ground cumin

1/4 tsp. salt
4 flour tortillas, about 10 inches in diameter
1 cup shredded pepper Jack cheese
1/2 cup shredded fresh spinach leaves

Prepare a medium-hot grill. For Salsa Cruda, combine tomatoes, onion, cilantro, cumin and salt in a medium bowl. Let stand for 10 minutes to allow flavors to blend. Sprinkle 1/2 cup shredded cheese on a tortilla. Keep cheese within 1 inch of the edge. Scatter 1/4 cup spinach over cheese. Repeat with a second tortilla. Top with remaining tortillas. Grill quesadillas for about 2 minutes. Carefully flip and continue grilling for an additional 2 minutes, until lightly browned on each side. Cut each quesadilla into quarters. Serve immediately and garnish with *Salsa Cruda.*

GRILLED CRAB QUESADILLAS

Substitute 1 cup cooked, flaked crabmeat for the spinach.

GRILLED CHICKEN QUESADILLAS

Substitute 1 cup cooked, shredded chicken for the spinach.

ROSEMARY CHICKEN SKEWERS

Try a crisp Chardonnay in this dish; it mingles well with the herbs and garlic. If using bamboo skewers, soak them in water for a half-hour before using to keep them from scorching.

4 boneless, skinless chicken breasts, cut into 2-inch chunks
2 cloves garlic, minced, divided
1/4 tsp. pepper

1 1/2 tsp. chopped fresh rosemary, divided
1/4 cup plus 2 tbs. dry white wine, divided
1/4 cup butter
1/4 tsp. salt

In a medium bowl, combine chicken, 1 clove of the garlic, pepper, 1 tsp. of the rosemary and 1/4 cup of the wine; toss to coat. Cover bowl and marinate for 4 hours in the refrigerator or 1/2 hour at room temperature. Prepare a medium-hot grill. Thread several pieces of chicken on each skewer and grill until about 10 minutes until cooked through, turning often. Combine remaining 2 tbs. wine, remaining 1/2 tsp. rosemary, remaining 1 clove garlic and salt in a small saucepan. Bring to a boil over medium heat. Drizzle chicken skewers with sauce. Serve immediately.

BASIL OR TARRAGON CHICKEN SKEWERS
Substitute fresh tarragon or basil for the rosemary in the marinade and sauce.

ROSEMARY PORK SKEWERS
Substitute 1 lb. pork loin, cubed, for the chicken breasts.

LEMON-HERB SHRIMP

You can skewer the shrimp and mix up the sauce early in the day, as long as you keep them tightly wrapped in the refrigerator. Pour the sauce over the shrimp when you are ready to serve.

2 tbs. minced fresh chives
2 tbs. finely chopped fresh parsley
juice of 2 lemons
grated zest of 1 lemon
1 tbs. Dijon-style mustard

1/4 cup olive oil
2 tbs. vegetable oil
1/4 tsp. pepper
1/4 tsp. salt
2 lb. large shrimp, cooked and peeled

In a medium bowl, combine chives, parsley, lemon juice, lemon zest, mustard, olive oil, vegetable oil, pepper and salt. Stir to mix well. Add shrimp to bowl and stir to coat all shrimp evenly with marinade. Thread 3 or 4 shrimp onto each bamboo skewer and serve immediately.

LEMON-HERB SCALLOPS

Substitute 2 lb. cooked sea scallops for the shrimp.

LEMON-HERB CRAB LEGS

Transfer lemon-herb mixture to a small serving bowl. Substitute 4 lb. cooked crab legs for shrimp; do not add crab legs to lemon-herb mixture. Serve crab legs on a platter with lemon-herb mixture for dipping.

SHRIMP WITH LEMON AIOLI

Aioli is a rich mayonnaise-like dipping sauce that goes wonderfully with seafood. Raw eggs can cause salmonella; use Egg Beaters if you're concerned.

8 cloves garlic
juice and grated zest of 1 lemon
2 egg yolks, or 1/4 cup Egg Beaters

1/2 cup vegetable oil
1/2 cup olive oil
1 1/2 lb. large shrimp, cooked and peeled

In a blender container, combine garlic, lemon juice, zest and egg yolks. Pulse until smooth and light yellow in color. Combine vegetable oil and olive oil. Turn blender on high and slowly pour oil in a steady stream; gradually increase the amount of oil poured as the mixture thickens. Do not let oil pool. Remove aioli from blender and place in a bowl with a tight-fitting lid. Refrigerate for 3 to 4 hours to let flavors blend. Keep refrigerated until ready to use. Place shrimp on a serving platter and serve with aioli.

SHRIMP WITH LEMON-CAPER AIOLI

Add 2 tbs. drained and rinsed capers to the aioli.

SHRIMP WITH LEMON-PEPPERCORN AIOLI

Add 2 tbs. drained and rinsed green peppercorns to the aioli.

POACHED SALMON WITH
SWEET RED PEPPER SAUCE

Servings: 8–10

This can be served as a buffet appetizer, a first course or a light summer entrée. The red of the bell pepper dressing complements the pink of the salmon and makes a lovely presentation.

1 salmon fillet, 3–4 lb.
½ cup cider vinegar
½ cup minced red bell pepper

3 tbs. capers, rinsed
1 clove garlic, minced
½ tsp. salt

Place salmon in a large poaching rack or steamer. Add water to pan to about ½ inch below top of fish. Bring water to a boil over high heat. Reduce heat to low, cover and simmer for 20 to 30 minutes, or until salmon flakes easily when tested with a fork. Transfer salmon to a serving platter. Cover and refrigerate until chilled. In a small bowl, combine vinegar, bell pepper, capers, garlic and salt. Cover and refrigerate for at least 30 minutes. To serve, spoon sauce over salmon.

POACHED SALMON WITH SHALLOT-CHIVE SAUCE

Substitute ¼ cup each minced shallots and minced chives for the red peppers and capers.

POACHED SALMON WITH DILL-GREEN ONION SAUCE

Substitute ¼ cup minced green onions and 1 tbs. fresh chopped dill for the red peppers and capers.

CLASSIC CRAB CAKES

You can make these crab cakes as appetizers, a main course or even as an addition to a salad. To make them as appetizers or for a salad, shape them into patties about 2 inches in diameter.

½ lb. cooked crabmeat
¾ cup fresh breadcrumbs
1 egg, beaten
2 tbs. mayonnaise

¾ tsp. Old Bay Seasoning
¼ tsp. grated lemon zest
2 tbs. butter

In a large bowl, combine crabmeat, breadcrumbs, egg, mayonnaise, Old Bay and lemon zest. Form mixture into four ½-inch-thick patties. Heat butter in a large skillet over medium heat. Add crab cakes and cook 4 to 5 minutes per side until golden brown. Serve immediately.

CLASSIC SHRIMP CAKES
Substitute cooked chopped shrimp for the crabmeat.

CLASSIC SALMON CAKES
Substitute cooked, flaked salmon for the crabmeat.

SALADS

SIMPLY PERFECT SALAD

A tossed green salad with a light vinaigrette is simply a perfect accompaniment to any meal. This salad can be dressed up with different vegetables and lettuces.

1/3 cup cider vinegar	1/8 tsp. pepper
1 tbs. Dijon-style mustard	3/4 cup vegetable oil
1 clove garlic, minced	4 cups torn romaine lettuce leaves
3/4 tsp. salt	grated Parmesan cheese, optional

In a small bowl, whisk together vinegar, mustard, garlic, salt and pepper. Whisk in oil. Set aside. In a large bowl, place romaine and drizzle dressing over greens to taste. (You will have dressing left over. Store dressing in a covered container for up to 2 weeks in refrigerator.) Toss to mix and serve. Sprinkle Parmesan cheese on top, if desired.

SIMPLY PERFECT SUMMER SALAD

Thinly slice 2 large ripe beefsteak tomatoes and arrange slices on top of each salad plate. Drizzle a bit more dressing over tomatoes.

SIMPLY PERFECT VEGETABLE SALAD

Substitute 1 cup each thinly sliced zucchini, thinly sliced carrots, thinly sliced green bell peppers and thinly sliced sweet red onion for the romaine.

ARTICHOKE AND TOMATO SALAD

Servings: 4-6

Perfect for a special dinner or a casual picnic, this salad can be assembled early in the day and tossed with the dressing just before serving.

1 cup canned baby corn
4 cups coarsely chopped tomatoes
2 jars (7.5 oz. each) artichoke hearts, coarsely chopped
1/2 cup chopped green onions
1 cup olive oil

1/2 cup cider vinegar
1/2 tsp. salt
grated zest of 1 lemon
1/4 tsp. dried oregano
1/4 tsp. dried basil
1/4 tsp. dried thyme

Cut baby corn into 1/2-inch thick slices and place in a large bowl. Add tomatoes, artichoke hearts and green onions; stir to combine. In a medium bowl, whisk together oil, vinegar, salt, zest, oregano, basil and thyme. Pour dressing over salad and toss well. Serve immediately.

TOMATO AND HEARTS OF PALM SALAD

Substitute 2 cans (14 oz. each) hearts of palm, cut into 1/2 slices, for the artichoke hearts. Omit baby corn.

GREEK ARTICHOKE AND TOMATO SALAD

Add 1/2 cup crumbled feta cheese and 1/2 cup pitted kalamata olives.

GRILLED VEGETABLE SALAD

More of a side dish than a true salad, this lively combination makes a lovely presentation.

1/4 cup olive oil

1/4 tsp. dried basil

1/4 tsp. pepper

3 medium zucchini, sliced lengthwise in thirds

4 stalks celery, cut in half lengthwise

1 yellow onion, sliced 1/2-inch thick

1 green bell pepper, seeded, halved

2 tbs. balsamic vinegar

1 tbs. capers

1/4 tsp. salt

Early in the day, combine oil, basil and pepper in a small container. Let stand at room temperature for at least 4 hours. Prepare a medium-hot grill. Combine zucchini, celery, onion and bell pepper in a large bowl. Add seasoned oil and toss gently to coat. Grill vegetables until crisp-tender, turning once: about 6 minutes for zucchini; about 2 minutes for celery, onion and green pepper. Reserve seasoned oil. Cut vegetables into bite-sized pieces. In a small bowl, combine reserved oil, vinegar, capers and salt and pour over vegetables. Toss gently to coat.

GRILLED EGGPLANT AND VEGETABLE SALAD

Substitute 1 medium unpeeled eggplant, sliced 1/2-inch thick, for the zucchini.

HERBED GRILLED VEGETABLE SALAD

Add 1/4 tsp. dried oregano and 1 clove garlic, minced, to oil along with the basil.

MEDITERRANEAN COBB SALAD

Like the classic cobb salad, this dish displays the delicious additions in colorful rows on top of the lettuce, rather than mixed in. This version of cobb salad features feta rather than the more traditional blue cheese. Pancetta is a cured unsmoked Italian bacon. Look for it in Italian delis or specialty food stores.

¼ cup balsamic vinegar
⅓ cup olive oil
¼ tsp. salt
¼ tsp. pepper
6 cups torn romaine lettuce
4 hard-cooked eggs, peeled and chopped
¾ cup crumbled feta cheese
1 cup cooked chopped pancetta
1½ cups chopped tomatoes
½ cup pitted kalamata olives
½ cup roasted red bell peppers, chopped

In a small bowl, whisk together vinegar, oil, salt and pepper; set aside. Place romaine on a large serving platter. Top with a row each of eggs, feta, pancetta, tomatoes, olives and roasted red peppers. Pour dressing over salad just before serving. Toss salad, if desired.

SOUTHWESTERN COBB SALAD

Substitute 3 tbs. cider vinegar for the balsamic vinegar in the dressing. Substitute shredded pepper Jack cheese for the feta. Substitute 1 cup sliced smoked chicken breast for the pancetta. Substitute fresh or frozen corn kernels, thawed, for the kalamata olives.

SAN FRANCISCO COBB SALAD

Substitute 3/4 cup shredded cheddar for the feta. Substitute 1 cup cooked crabmeat for the pancetta. Substitute 1 cup cubed avocado for the kalamata olives and red peppers.

ASIAN NOODLE SALAD

This cold pasta salad can be made any time of year. Substitute a jar of roasted red peppers if fresh ones are not in season.

¼ cup rice vinegar
1 tbs. sesame oil
½ cup vegetable oil
1 tsp. soy sauce
1 clove garlic, minced

1 lb. fresh or dried angel hair pasta
1 cup shredded carrots
½ cup chopped green onions
½ cup chopped snow pea pods
¾ cup thinly sliced red bell peppers

In a small bowl, whisk together vinegar, sesame oil, vegetable oil, soy sauce and garlic. Set aside. Cook pasta in a large pot of boiling salted water according to package directions. Rinse with cool water and drain. Place pasta in a large bowl and add carrots, green onions, pea pods and bell peppers. Pour dressing over pasta and vegetables; toss to mix. Serve at room temperature or refrigerate and serve chilled.

THAI PEANUT NOODLE SALAD
Add 2 tbs. smooth peanut butter and 1tsp. crushed red pepper flakes to the dressing.

ASIAN NOODLE SALAD WITH CHICKEN
Add 1½ cups cooked chopped chicken along with the vegetables.

GREEK-STYLE COUSCOUS SALAD

Tiny grains of pasta called couscous cook quickly: all you need to do is pour boiling water over them. Here couscous is livened up with components of a classic Greek salad.

2 cups cooked couscous, cooled
½ cup diced cucumber
½ cup diced tomatoes
¼ cup coarsely chopped pitted kalamata olives
2 tbs. crumbled feta cheese

⅔ cup olive oil
¼ cup red wine vinegar
¼ tsp. dried oregano
⅛ tsp. salt
⅛ tsp. pepper

In a medium bowl, combine couscous, cucumber, tomatoes, olives and feta. In a separate bowl, whisk together oil, vinegar, oregano, salt and pepper. Pour dressing over salad. Stir well to combine. Refrigerate until cold.

GREEK-STYLE COUSCOUS SALAD WITH SUN-DRIED TOMATOES
Substitute ¼ cup finely chopped sun-dried tomatoes for the diced tomatoes.

ITALIAN-STYLE COUSCOUS SALAD
Substitute 2 tbs. shredded Parmesan cheese for the feta. Add ¼ cup pine nuts.

CAESAR TORTELLINI SALAD

The bright flavors of a Caesar salad make an interesting dressing for this pasta salad. Use more garlic or anchovies if you are feeling adventurous.

3 cloves garlic
1/2 cup olive oil
3 tbs. fresh lemon juice
1 tsp. grated lemon zest

6 anchovies
1 lb. fresh or frozen tortellini
1/4 cup grated Parmesan cheese

Combine garlic, oil, lemon juice, lemon zest and anchovies in a blender container. Pulse until smooth and set aside. Cook tortellini in boiling salted water according to package directions. Rinse in cold water to cool and drain well. In a large bowl, combine tortellini and dressing. Toss to mix. Sprinkle Parmesan over pasta and toss again.

ROMAINE AND TORTELLINI SALAD
Serve completed salad on top of 4 cups torn romaine lettuce.

CAESAR PASTA SALAD
Substitute any pasta shape for the tortellini.

SPINACH AND BACON SALAD

This version of a classic spinach salad features a simple vinaigrette instead of the usual sweet and sour hot dressing.

4 cups fresh spinach leaves, well washed and
   dried
1 hard-cooked egg, peeled and sliced
1/3 cup sliced sweet red onion
1/2 cup sliced white mushrooms

2 tbs. cooked, crumbled bacon
1/4 cup olive oil
1 tbs. red wine vinegar
1 1/2 tbs. balsamic vinegar

In a large bowl, combine spinach, egg, onion, mushrooms and bacon. In a small bowl, whisk together oil, wine vinegar and balsamic vinegar. Drizzle dressing over salad, toss to coat and serve immediately.

SPINACH AND CHEESE SALAD
   Add 1/4 cup shredded Swiss cheese.

ITALIAN SPINACH SALAD
   Add 1/4 cup shredded Parmesan. Substitute 1/4 cup minced, cooked pancetta for the bacon.

CASHEW CHICKEN SALAD

All the things you love in a Chinese cashew chicken entrée are disguised as a light salad.

4 boneless, skinless chicken breast halves, cooked and chopped
1/2 cup cashew pieces
1/2 cup shredded carrots
1/4 cup chopped green onions
1/2 cup coarsely chopped water chestnuts

1/2 cup rice vinegar
1/2 cup vegetable oil
1/2 tsp. sesame oil
1/2 tsp. ground ginger
1/2 tsp. salt
4 cups shredded lettuce

In a large bowl, combine chicken, cashews, carrots, green onions and water chestnuts. Stir to mix; set aside. In a small bowl, whisk together vinegar, vegetable oil, sesame oil, ginger and salt. Pour dressing over salad and toss. Serve over shredded lettuce.

ALMOND CHICKEN SALAD
Substitute slivered almonds for the cashews.

CASHEW TURKEY SALAD
Substitute 1 large cooked skinless turkey breast, chopped, for the chicken.

CREAMY CASHEW CHICKEN SALAD
Substitute 1 cup mayonnaise for the vinegar and oils. Increase ginger to 3/4 tsp.

CURRIED CHICKEN SALAD

This salad has all the flavor without the heat found in most curry dishes. It is a hearty salad, suitable for a luncheon entrée or sandwich filling.

2 medium-sized red potatoes, unpeeled
2 skinless chicken breast halves, cooked and
  chopped
$\frac{1}{2}$ cup chopped celery
3 tbs. minced green onions

$\frac{2}{3}$ cup raisins
$1\frac{1}{3}$ cups mayonnaise
3 tbs. red wine vinegar
$\frac{1}{2}$ tsp. salt
5 tsp. curry powder

Place potatoes in a small pot. Add water to cover and cook on high heat until boiling. Reduce heat to medium and cook for about 20 minutes, or until potatoes are tender. Drain potatoes and cool. Cut potatoes into $\frac{1}{2}$-inch cubes. In a large bowl, combine potatoes, chicken, celery, onions and raisins. In a small bowl, whisk together mayonnaise, vinegar, salt and curry powder. Add to chicken mixture. Stir well, cover and refrigerate until chilled. Serve in sandwiches or on lettuce.

CURRIED TURKEY SALAD

Substitute 3 cups cooked chopped turkey for the chicken.

CHICKEN AND POTATO SALAD

Omit raisins and curry powder.

SOUPS

FRESH TOMATO SOUP

This is the perfect soup to make in late summer when fresh tomatoes are abundant. Once you see how easy it is to make fresh soup, you will never want to eat soup from a can again.

¼ cup (½ stick) butter
1 yellow onion, chopped
4 cups chopped fresh tomatoes

¼ tsp. pepper
1 tsp. salt
½ cup chicken broth

In a stockpot, melt butter over medium-high heat. Add onion and sauté until onion just begins to brown. Add tomatoes, pepper, salt and broth. Bring to a boil; cover and reduce heat to low. Simmer for 20 minutes. Pour (in batches if necessary) into a blender container or food processor workbowl and puree. Return to pot and heat to boiling. Serve immediately.

FRESH TOMATO AND BASIL SOUP

After pureeing soup, add ¼ cup chopped fresh basil and bring to a boil.

FRESH TOMATO AND LEEK SOUP

Substitute 2 thinly sliced large leeks for the onion.

FRESH HEIRLOOM TOMATO SOUP

Substitute yellow plum tomatoes (or other heirloom tomato) for the tomatoes.

GAZPACHO (COLD SPANISH SOUP)

Servings: 4

This simple Spanish-style chilled soup called gazpacho has hundreds of variations. It makes a perfect summer meal on a hot day — serve it with chips, guacamole and a pitcher of sangria.

1 cup chopped celery
1 cup peeled chopped cucumbers
2/3 cup chopped red onion
2 cups chopped tomatoes
1 cup chopped green bell peppers

1 tsp. ground cumin
1/2 tsp. pepper
1/2 tsp. salt
3 cups vegetable juice, such as V-8

In a large bowl, combine all ingredients, stirring well. Refrigerate for 30 minutes; serve cold.

BLENDED GAZPACHO

After combining ingredients, pour soup into a blender container and pulse until vegetables are finely chopped: soup should not be smooth. Refrigerate and serve chilled.

CRAB GAZPACHO

Just before serving, add 1 cup cooked crabmeat to soup.

SHRIMP GAZPACHO

Just before serving, add 1 cup cooked chopped shrimp to soup.

ASIAN VEGETABLE SOUP

Asian vegetables in a light broth make an excellent first course for any day of the week. Bok choy, also called Chinese cabbage, is a type of cabbage common to Asian cookery. Enoki mushrooms are long, delicate white mushrooms. Look for both in grocery stores, Asian markets or specialty food stores.

6 cups chicken broth
1 tsp. soy sauce
1/4 cup dry sherry
1/2 cup thinly sliced bok choy

4 oz. enoki mushrooms
4 oz. snow pea pods, sliced
1 egg, beaten
2 green onions, chopped

In a large saucepan, combine broth, soy sauce, sherry, bok choy, mushrooms and snow peas. Bring soup to a boil. Stirring soup constantly, slowly pour egg into soup.s Ladle soup into bowls and sprinkle green onions on top. Serve immediately.

ASIAN VEGETABLE SOUP WITH TOFU

Add 1/2 cup cubed tofu along with the vegetables.

ASIAN VEGETABLE SOUP WITH SHRIMP

Add 1/2 cup cooked chopped shrimp along with the vegetables.

AUTUMN SOUP

Serve this a first course soup or as a light meal. If you can't find fresh pumpkin, substitute 2 cups of unseasoned canned pumpkin, and add it when the other vegetables are tender.

1/4 cup (1/2 stick) butter
1 yellow onion, chopped
4 cups peeled chopped fresh pumpkin
2 large potatoes, peeled and chopped
4 carrots, chopped
4 medium turnips, chopped

4 cups chicken broth
1/3 cup sherry
1/4 tsp. ground nutmeg
1/2 tsp. salt
2 cups half-and-half

In a stockpot, melt butter over medium heat. Add onion and sauté until translucent. Add pumpkin, potatoes, carrots and turnips and sauté until onion begins to turn golden. Add broth and bring mixture to a boil. Reduce heat to low, cover and simmer about 30 minutes until vegetables are tender. Puree mixture in 2 or 3 batches in a blender container or food processor workbowl. Return pureed soup to pot. Add sherry, nutmeg and salt. Bring to a boil over medium-high heat, stirring frequently. Remove from heat, stir in half-and-half and serve immediately.

AUTUMN HONEY AND PUMPKIN SOUP

Omit turnips and add ¼ cup honey along with the broth.

WINTER VEGETABLE SOUP

Substitute peeled, seeded, chopped butternut, acorn or banana squash for the pumpkin.

SPRING VEGETABLE SOUP

Omit pumpkin and turnips. After you have pureed soup, add 3 cups chopped baby yellow squash and bring mixture to a boil. Reduce heat and simmer only until squash is tender. Add half-and-half and serve.

BUTTERNUT SQUASH SOUP

Top servings of this favorite autumn soup with crunchy homemade croutons.

1 tbs. butter
1 yellow onion, chopped
1 butternut squash (about 2 lb.), peeled,
    seeded and cut into 1-inch cubes

3 cups chicken broth
1/4 tsp. salt
1/2 cup heavy cream

In a stockpot, melt butter over medium-high heat. Add onion and cook until translucent. Add squash, chicken broth and salt. Bring mixture to a boil. Reduce heat to low and simmer uncovered for 30 minutes or until squash is soft. Puree soup (in batches if necessary) in a blender container. Return soup to pot and bring to a boil. Remove from heat and stir in cream.

APPLE BUTTERNUT SQUASH SOUP
Add 1 large peeled, chopped Granny Smith apple along with the squash.

BUTTERNUT SQUASH SOUP (LOW-FAT VERSION)
Add 1 medium peeled, chopped potato along with the squash. Omit cream.

CURRIED BUTTERNUT SQUASH SOUP
Add 1 tsp. curry powder, or to taste, along with the squash.

GOLDEN MUSHROOM SOUP

Browning the mushrooms gives this soup its golden color.

½ cup (1 stick) butter
8 cups coarsely chopped fresh white
   mushrooms
1 large yellow onion, chopped

2 cups chicken broth
½ cup dry sherry
½ tsp. salt
1 cup half-and-half

In a stockpot, melt butter over medium-high heat. Add mushrooms and onion. Sauté over medium-high heat, stirring very frequently, until mushrooms turn a golden brown. Add broth, sherry and salt. Bring to a boil over medium-high heat. Reduce heat to low and simmer uncovered for 15 minutes. Remove from heat, add half-and-half and serve immediately.

MIXED MUSHROOM SOUP

Reduce white mushrooms to 4 cups. Add 1 cup each chopped shiitake, oyster and portobello mushrooms, and ½ oz. dried porcini mushrooms, rehydrated in ½ cup boiling water for 20 minutes. Substitute white wine for the sherry. Simmer for 20 minutes.

GOLDEN MUSHROOM AND POTATO SOUP

Add 2 peeled, chopped potatoes. Increase broth to 3 cups and simmer for 20 minutes. Increase cream to 1½ cups.

CREAM OF ARTICHOKE SOUP

Every year in Watsonville, California, there is an artichoke festival where you can try artichoke soup in many forms. Here is just one of several creations.

2 tsp. butter
1 yellow onion, chopped
4 cups drained canned artichoke hearts (do not use marinated)

1 large russet potato, peeled and chopped
3 cups chicken broth
1 tsp. salt
1 cup half-and-half

In a stockpot, melt butter over medium heat. Add onion and sauté until onion is translucent. Add artichoke hearts, potato, broth and salt. Bring mixture to a boil, reduce heat to low and simmer for 15 minutes, or until potatoes are tender. Remove from heat and cool slightly. Puree soup (in batches if necessary) in a blender container. Return soup to stockpot and bring to a boil. Remove from heat and stir in half and half. Serve immediately.

CREAM OF BROCCOLI OR ASPARAGUS SOUP

Substitute chopped broccoli or asparagus for the artichoke hearts.

CREAM OF CARROT SOUP

Substitute chopped carrots for the artichoke hearts.

FIERY CREAM OF RED PEPPER SOUP

When red bell peppers are in season and inexpensive, take advantage and stock up. Seed them, quarter them and freeze them in plastic bags and you can enjoy this soup any time.

2 tbs. butter
1 yellow onion, chopped
3 large red bell peppers, seeded and chopped
2 cups chicken broth

$\frac{1}{2}$ tsp. ground cumin
$\frac{1}{2}$ tsp. salt
$\frac{1}{4}$ tsp. cayenne pepper, or more to taste
$\frac{1}{2}$ cup heavy cream

In a stockpot, melt butter over medium-high heat. Add chopped onion and sauté until translucent, about 5 minutes. Add peppers and broth to onions and bring to a boil. Reduce heat and simmer about 15 minutes until peppers are soft. Remove from heat. Puree soup in a blender container until smooth and return to pot. Add cumin, salt and cayenne. Bring soup to a boil, reduce heat to low and simmer for 5 minutes, stirring frequently. Remove from heat. Stir cream into soup.

FIERY CREAM OF YELLOW PEPPER SOUP
Substitute yellow bell peppers for the red peppers.

CREAM OF ROASTED RED PEPPER SOUP
Place whole peppers under a broiler to char skin; then place in a paper bag. Let peppers stand for 5 minutes. Remove blackened skin, chop peppers, and add to soup along with the broth.

ROASTED CORN CHOWDER

Servings: 6–8

Roasting the corn adds a smoky flavor to this chowder. You can use fresh corn instead.

4 ears fresh corn, husks and silk removed
8 cups water
1 large potato, peeled and chopped
2 small red-skinned potatoes, chopped

1 yellow onion, chopped
1 cup chopped celery
1½ tsp. salt
1 cup milk

Prepare a medium-hot grill. Grill corn, turning frequently, just until it begins to brown. Set aside to cool. Cut corn kernels from cobs, reserving cobs. In a stockpot, combine corncobs, water and peeled potato. Bring to a boil over high heat, reduce heat to low, cover and simmer for 30 minutes. Remove and discard cobs. Puree cooked potato and 2 cups of the corn stock in a blender container. Return puree to the stockpot. Add corn kernels, red potatoes, onion, celery and salt. Bring soup to a boil and reduce heat to low. Simmer uncovered for 20 minutes or until potatoes are tender and soup is thickened. Remove from heat. Stir in milk and serve immediately.

ROASTED CORN AND SAUSAGE OR RED PEPPER CHOWDER

Add 1 cup chopped, cooked sausage or roasted red peppers along with the corn kernels.

SPRING VEGETABLE AND ROASTED CORN CHOWDER

Add 1½ cups chopped summer squash and 1 cup chopped carrots along with the corn kernels.

BLACK BEAN SOUP WITH SAUSAGE

The smoky flavor of the sausage and bacon helps create a complex set of flavors in this soup.

6 slices bacon

1 yellow onion, chopped

3 cans (15 oz. each) black beans, rinsed and drained. divided

2 cans (14½ oz. each) chicken broth, divided

1½ cups sliced cooked smoked sausage

1 cup corn kernels

1 cup chopped carrots

1 cup chopped celery

½ tsp. pepper

In a stockpot, cook bacon over medium-high heat until crisp. Drain all but 1 tbs. fat from pot. Crumble bacon and set aside. Return pot to heat and add onion. Sauté until translucent. Puree 2 cans of the beans and 1 can of the broth in a blender container. Add to cooked onions in stockpot. Add remaining beans and remaining broth to pot. Add bacon, sausage, corn, carrots, celery and pepper. Bring soup to a boil. Reduce heat to low and cover. Simmer for 30 minutes.

BLACK BEAN SOUP WITH HAM

Substitute chopped ham for the sausage.

ARIZONA BLACK BEAN SOUP

Add 1 chipotle pepper (seeded and chopped), ¾ tsp. cumin and 1 cup chopped red bell pepper along with the sausage and bacon.

ITALIAN MEATBALL SOUP

Servings: 6–8

Some restaurants call this filling dish "Italian Wedding Soup." It's great with sourdough bread.

¾ lb. ground beef
¼ lb. bulk Italian sausage
½ cup dry breadcrumbs
2 eggs
1 yellow onion, chopped
8 cups beef broth

½ tsp. dried oregano
2 cups chopped peeled tomatoes
2 carrots, chopped
2 stalks celery, chopped
2 cups chopped fresh Swiss chard or kale

In a medium bowl, mix together ground beef, sausage, breadcrumbs and eggs. Shape into 1-inch meatballs. Heat a stockpot over medium heat. Add meatballs and cook until lightly browned. Remove meatballs and set aside; drain excess fat from pot. Return pot to stove, add onion and sauté until translucent. Add broth, oregano, tomatoes, carrots, celery and Swiss chard and increase heat to high. Bring mixture to a boil; reduce heat to low. Add meatballs and simmer for 20 minutes.

ITALIAN MEATBALL AND TORTELLINI SOUP
Add ¼ lb. cooked tortellini just before serving.

ITALIAN TORTELLINI SOUP
Substitute 1 lb. tortellini, cooked, for the meatballs.

SHRIMP BISQUE

Bisques usually contain seafood and cream. This version uses tomatoes for a creamy red color.

¼ cup (½ stick) butter
2 stalks celery, chopped
½ yellow onion, chopped
½ cup dry white wine
6 cups chicken or vegetable broth
½ cup uncooked white rice

2 cups peeled chopped fresh tomatoes
1 tsp. salt
¼ tsp. cayenne pepper
1 lb. medium shrimp, cooked and peeled
1 cup heavy cream

In a stockpot, melt butter over medium heat. Add celery and onion and sauté until vegetables are tender. Add wine, broth, rice, tomatoes, salt and cayenne. Bring to a boil, cover and reduce heat to low. Simmer for 20 minutes, or until rice is tender. Puree (in batches if necessary) in a blender container until smooth. Return to pot and bring to a boil. Stir in shrimp and cream and serve immediately (do not let soup boil once cream has been added).

CRAB OR LOBSTER BISQUE
Substitute cooked crabmeat or cooked lobster meat for the shrimp.

SEAFOOD BISQUE
Reduce shrimp to ½ lb; add ⅓ lb. each cooked crabmeat and cooked lobster meat.

SIDE DISHES

BROCCOLI WITH SESAME BUTTER

Servings: 4–6

Vegetables cooked tender-crisp need only the simplest sauce to complement their flavors. Here, sesame butter adds an Asian touch to steamed fresh broccoli.

1 lb. broccoli florets
1 tsp. sesame seeds
¼ cup (½ stick) butter

4 tsp. soy sauce
½ tsp. sesame oil

In a steamer or covered saucepan with a steamer insert, steam broccoli until tender-crisp. Meanwhile, place a small skillet over medium heat. Add sesame seeds and sauté until light golden brown, stirring constantly to prevent burning. Remove from skillet and set aside. Melt butter in a small saucepan over medium heat. Stir in soy sauce and sesame oil and remove from heat. Drain broccoli, pour butter sauce over and toss to coat. Sprinkle broccoli with toasted sesame seeds.

SUGAR SNAP PEAS WITH SESAME BUTTER
Substitute sugar snap peas for broccoli florets.

ZUCCHINI WITH SESAME BUTTER
Substitute sliced zucchini for broccoli florets.

BABY BOK CHOY WITH SESAME BUTTER
Substitute sliced baby bok choy for broccoli florets.

OVEN-ROASTED TOMATOES

Roasting tomatoes makes their flavor much more intense. Roma tomatoes are a perfect choice for this recipe because they have a lot of tomato flesh for their size and few seeds.

4 ripe Roma tomatoes
2 tsp. olive oil

Heat oven to 250°. Slice tomatoes in half lengthwise. Place tomatoes, skin side down, on a cookie sheet. Drizzle $1/4$ tsp. of the olive oil over each tomato half. Place pan in oven. Roast for 3 hours and serve immediately.

OREGANO- OR BASIL-ROASTED TOMATOES

After drizzling oil, sprinkle $1/8$ tsp. crumbled, dried oregano or basil (or $1/4$ tsp. fresh) on each half.

TARRAGON-ROASTED TOMATOES

After drizzling oil, sprinkle $1/8$ tsp. crumbled, dried tarragon (or $1/4$ tsp. fresh) on each half.

RATATOUILLE

Ratatouille is delicious hot or cold. Vary the vegetables to your personal style.

1 eggplant, peeled and cubed
½ tsp. salt
2 tbs. olive oil
2 cloves garlic, chopped
1 yellow onion, chopped
1 green bell pepper, seeded and chopped

2 stalks celery, sliced
4 cups peeled tomatoes with juice
¼ cup chopped fresh Italian parsley
¼ tsp. dried thyme
2 bay leaves
½ cup red wine

Place eggplant in a colander and sprinkle with salt. Set aside for 20 minutes. Heat oil in a large pot over medium-high heat. Add garlic and onion and sauté until they begin to brown. Add eggplant, bell pepper, celery, tomatoes, parsley, thyme, bay leaves and wine. Bring to a boil, reduce heat to low, cover and simmer for 20 minutes. Remove bay leaves before serving.

CHICKEN RATATOUILLE

Add 2 cups chopped or sliced cooked chicken about 5 minutes before serving.

SHRIMP RATATOUILLE

Add 2 cups cooked chopped shrimp about 5 minutes before serving.

BUTTERMILK MASHED POTATOES

The extra texture from these potatoes will remind you of the "homeyness" of the holidays. Using a hand masher helps keep these potatoes from becoming too smooth.

2½ lb. red-skinned potatoes
2 tbs. butter
1 cup buttermilk

¾ tsp. salt
½ tsp. pepper

Cut unpeeled potatoes into large chunks. Place in a large pot and add water to cover. Place on high heat and bring potatoes to a boil. Reduce heat to medium and cook until potatoes are tender.

Remove from heat and drain. In a large bowl, mash potatoes with a masher or a pastry cutter; potatoes should not be smooth, do not use a mixer. Add butter and stir until butter is melted. Stir in buttermilk, salt and pepper and mix well. Serve immediately.

SOUR CREAM MASHED POTATOES

Substitute sour cream for the buttermilk.

SOUR CREAM AND CHIVE MASHED POTATOES

Substitute sour cream for the buttermilk. Add ½ cup minced chives.

BUTTERMILK AND BACON MASHED POTATOES

Add ½ cup cooked crumbled bacon when you add the buttermilk.

DELICATE POTATO PANCAKES

Place the shredded potatoes in water to wash away some of the potato starch; this keeps the potato pancakes so light. Leave skins on the potatoes for a more rustic pancake, if you wish.

3 medium-sized baking potatoes, peeled
2 tbs. minced yellow onion
2 eggs, beaten
2 tbs. flour

1 tsp. salt
1/4 tsp. baking powder
vegetable shortening for frying

Fill a large bowl halfway with cold water. Shred potatoes into water and set aside while preparing batter. In a large bowl, mix together onion, eggs, flour, salt and baking powder. Drain potatoes in a colander, shaking to remove excess water. Stir potatoes into flour mixture. Heat 1 tbs. shortening in a large nonstick skillet or griddle over medium-high heat. Drop batter by 1/3-cupfuls in skillet and cook for 10 minutes per side or until deep golden brown, turning only once. Serve hot.

DELICATE CHEDDAR POTATO PANCAKES

Add 1/2 cup shredded extra-sharp cheddar cheese along with the potatoes.

DELICATE CARROT AND POTATO PANCAKES

Add 1/2 cup shredded carrots along with the potatoes.

MUSTARD ROASTED POTATOES

Oven-roasted potatoes are a classic side dish. With the addition of mustard and herbs, you have a side dish that can stand up to any pork, beef or chicken entrée.

1½ lb. red-skinned potatoes	2 tbs. grainy mustard
1 yellow onion, chopped	½ tsp. salt
2 tbs. olive oil	½ tsp. pepper

Heat oven to 400°. Spray a 9 x 9-inch baking pan with nonstick cooking spray. Scrub potatoes and cut into large chunks. Place potatoes in a large bowl. Add onion, oil, mustard, salt and pepper and toss to coat well. Turn mixture into prepared baking pan. Roast 45 to 60 minutes, stirring occasionally until potatoes are tender and browned.

ROSEMARY AND MUSTARD ROASTED POTATOES

Add 1 tbs. chopped fresh rosemary before roasting.

DIJON ROASTED POTATOES

Substitute Dijon-style mustard for the grainy mustard.

POLENTA

Polenta is served as a side dish in Italy, just as rice or potatoes are in this country. It is delicious served straight from the pot, or chilled, sliced and grilled.

4 cups chicken broth or water
2 tbs. butter

1 cup cornmeal (polenta)
½ tsp. salt

Heat oven to 350°. In a medium saucepan over high heat, bring broth and butter to a boil. Remove from heat and stir in cornmeal and salt. Turn into a 2-quart covered casserole dish, cover and place in oven. Bake for 25 minutes. Remove from oven, stir and serve.

HERBED POLENTA

Stir in ¾ tsp. dried basil and ¾ tsp. dried oregano before placing in oven.

GARLIC POLENTA

In a small skillet, melt 1 tbs. butter over medium heat. Add 2 cloves garlic, minced. Sauté until garlic just begins to brown, about 3 minutes. Stir garlic and butter into polenta before placing in oven.

SUN-DRIED TOMATO POLENTA

Add 2 tbs. minced sun-dried tomatoes before placing in oven.

ARTICHOKE RICE

Subtly flavored, this rice can accompany some of your favorite bold-flavored main dishes. The wild rice variation adds a touch of elegance to your meal.

2 tbs. vegetable oil
1 cup long-grain rice
1 yellow onion, minced
2 cups water or vegetable broth

1⅓ cups chopped artichoke hearts
1 tsp. salt
½ tsp. pepper

In a large saucepan, heat oil over medium high heat. Add rice and sauté until rice turns translucent. Add onion and continue to sauté until rice begins to brown and onions are translucent, about 5 minutes. Add water or broth, artichoke hearts, salt and pepper. Bring mixture to a boil, reduce heat to low, cover and simmer until rice is tender, about 15 minutes. Serve immediately.

BROWN AND WILD ARTICHOKE RICE

Substitute ½ cup each brown rice and wild rice for the long-grain rice. Increase water to 2½ cups. Simmer 40 to 50 minutes, or until rice is tender.

ARTICHOKE AND PEPPER JACK RICE

Stir in 1 cup shredded pepper Jack cheese after rice has cooked.

FLORENTINE RICE

'Florentine' traditionally refers to a dish served on a bed of spinach, such as Eggs Florentine or Chicken Florentine. This colorful side dish makes a nice change from plain rice or potatoes on your dinner plate.

1 tbs. butter	1 pkg. (10 oz.) frozen chopped spinach,
1 yellow onion, minced	thawed and squeezed dry
1 cup long-grain rice	1/4 tsp. ground nutmeg
2 1/2 cups chicken broth, divided	1/2 tsp. salt

In a medium saucepan, melt butter over medium-high heat. Add onion; sauté until translucent. Add rice and 2 cups of the broth to saucepan. Increase heat to high and bring mixture to a boil, stirring occasionally. Reduce heat to low, cover and simmer for 15 minutes. Add remaining 1/2 cup broth, spinach, nutmeg and salt to rice. Stir to mix, cover and return to low heat. Continue to cook for another 5 to 8 minutes or until rice is tender, but not mushy. Serve immediately.

FLORENTINE PARMESAN RICE

Add 1 cup shredded Parmesan cheese just prior to serving.

SWISS CHARD RICE

Substitute 1 cup cooked red or green Swiss chard for the spinach.

VEGETABLE FRIED RICE

This side dish can be a full meal when teamed with a light soup. Fried rice is best when you use rice that was cooked the day before.

2 tbs. vegetable oil, divided
2 eggs, beaten
1 yellow onion, chopped
2 carrots, chopped
3 stalks celery, chopped

1 cup chopped fresh white mushrooms
4 cups cooked white rice
1 tbs. soy sauce
1 cup sliced snow pea pods

In a wok or a large skillet, heat 1 tsp. of the oil over medium heat. Pour eggs into wok and scramble eggs until done. Remove from wok; set aside. Heat 2 tsp. of the oil in wok. Add onion, carrots, celery and mushrooms. Stir-fry on high heat until vegetables are crisp-tender. Remove from wok and set aside. Heat remaining 1 tbs. oil in wok on high heat. Add rice and stir-fry until hot. Add soy sauce and toss to mix well. Add cooked egg, cooked vegetables and pea pods to rice. Stir fry on high heat until pea pods are tender-crisp.

CHICKEN, PORK OR SHRIMP FRIED RICE
Add 1 cup cooked, chopped chicken, pork or shrimp when adding pea pods.

CHORIZO RICE

This variation of Spanish rice uses Mexican chorizo sausage. Chorizo is available in bulk or in links. If using links, remove the sausage from casings before proceeding.

¾ lb. mild chorizo sausage
½ green bell pepper, seeded and chopped
3 cups chopped tomatoes
½ tsp. ground cumin

½ tsp. salt
1 cup long-grain white rice
1½ cups water or chicken broth

In a medium saucepan, crumble chorizo. Cook over medium-high heat until lightly browned. Drain all excess fat. Add bell pepper, tomatoes, cumin, salt, rice and water and stir to mix. Increase heat to high. Bring mixture to a boil, reduce heat to low, cover and simmer about 20 minutes until rice is tender.

WILDLY HOT AND SPICY CHORIZO RICE

Substitute ½ lb. hot chorizo for the mild chorizo. Add 1 can (4 oz.) chopped jalapeño peppers.

ITALIAN-STYLE SAUSAGE AND RICE

Substitute ½ lb. or or sweet Italian sausage for the mild chorizo . Substitute dried oregano or dried basil for the cumin.

PARMESAN RICE CAKES

These are an interesting departure from plain rice. They can be assembled early in the day and sautéed right before serving time.

2 cups cooked white rice
1/2 cup chopped fresh chives
1 cup fresh breadcrumbs
3 eggs

1/2 cup grated Parmesan cheese
3/4 tsp. salt
vegetable oil for frying

Combine rice, chives, breadcrumbs, eggs, Parmesan and salt. Form into 1/4 cup patties, pressing firmly. Heat 1 tbs. oil in a large skillet over medium heat. Place a few patties in skillet, making sure not to overcrowd. Saute about 5 minutes per side until golden. Keep warm while cooking remaining cakes. Add more oil as needed.

RICE CAKES

Omit Parmesan cheese.

PARMESAN BROWN RICE CAKES

Substitute cooked brown rice for the white rice.

PARMESAN WILD RICE CAKES

Substitute 1 cup of the white rice with 1 cup cooked wild rice.

BAKED PARMESAN RISOTTO

Though not a true risotto, this still uses the typical short-grained Arborio rice. You can make it a bit more true-to-form by stirring in ¹/₂ cup of hot chicken broth just before serving.

2 tbs. butter
1 cup Arborio rice
¹/₂ cup dry white wine

2 cups chicken broth
¹/₂ tsp. salt
¹/₂ cup grated Parmesan cheese

Heat oven to 400°. Spray sides and bottom of a large covered casserole dish with nonstick spray. In a medium saucepan over medium-high heat, melt butter. Add rice and stir constantly. Cook until rice begins to turn translucent, about 2 minutes. Add wine and stir until wine is absorbed. Add broth and salt and bring to a boil. Remove from heat and stir in Parmesan. Transfer to prepared casserole. Cover and bake for 35 minutes: rice should still be a bit firm. Serve immediately.

BAKED ROMANO RISOTTO

Substitute Romano cheese for the Parmesan.

BAKED CHEDDAR RISOTTO

Substitute sharp cheddar cheese for the Parmesan.

BAKED PARMESAN RISOTTO WITH CHIVES

Add ¹/₄ cup minced chives when you add the Parmesan.

RED CHARD RISOTTO

This risotto is full of flavorful Swiss chard, which turns it a light pink color. Regular green chard works just as well and will make a pretty green-flecked side dish.

5 cups chicken broth
2 tbs. olive oil
1 medium-sized yellow onion, minced
1½ cups Arborio rice

4 cups red Swiss chard, coarsely chopped
½ cup dry white wine
½ cup grated Parmesan cheese
salt to taste

Heat broth to just boiling in a saucepan. Lower heat and maintain a gentle simmer. Heat oil in a large saucepan over medium heat. Add onion and sauté for 2 to 3 minutes, until transparent. Add rice and Swiss chard and stir for 1 minute to thoroughly coat with oil. Add wine and stir constantly until wine is absorbed. Add ½ cup broth, stirring constantly until broth is absorbed. Continue to add broth ½ cup at a time, stirring frequently. It will take about 20 minutes to cook (it is best to have rice tender, but al dente). Use all the broth. Remove risotto from heat, stir in Parmesan and add salt to taste. Serve immediately.

SPINACH OR ARTICHOKE RISOTTO

Substitute 4 cups chopped fresh spinach or 2 cups chopped artichoke hearts for the Swiss chard.

FRESH HERB PASTA

This recipe is one great reason to grow an herb garden. Snip some fresh herbs as the pasta cooks and toss them into the finished dish. There is no easier, fresher way to present pasta.

12 oz. dried angel hair pasta
$1/3$ cup butter
2 tbs. olive oil
2 cloves garlic, minced

$1/4$ cup chopped fresh chives
$1/3$ cup chopped fresh Italian parsley
$1/2$ cup chopped fresh basil

Cook pasta in a large pot of boiling salted water according to package directions. In a small saucepan, melt butter over medium heat. Add olive oil and garlic. Cook over medium heat until garlic just begins to brown. Remove from heat. Drain pasta and place in a large serving bowl. Pour garlic butter over pasta and toss to coat. Add chives, parsley and basil. Toss to combine.

FRESH HERB AND CREAM PASTA
Omit butter; cook garlic in 2 tbs. olive oil. Remove from heat and add $1/2$ cup heavy cream. Add herbs and mix.

FRESH HERB AND PARMESAN PASTA
Add $1/2$ cup grated Parmesan cheese just before serving.

MAIN DISHES

PASTA PUTTANESCA

Servings: 4–6

This pasta sauce is fast and easy to prepare and it's full of summer flavors. You can use either peeled fresh tomatoes or canned tomatoes, depending on what you have on hand.

2 tbs. olive oil
2 cloves garlic, minced
1 yellow onion, chopped
2 tbs. capers, rinsed
4 cups chopped peeled fresh tomatoes

½ tsp. dried oregano
½ tsp. dried basil
½ tsp. salt
1 lb. linguini

In a large pot, heat oil over medium-high heat. Add garlic and onion and sauté for about 5 minutes, until onion begins to brown. Add capers, tomatoes, oregano, basil and salt and bring to a boil. Reduce heat to medium-low and simmer uncovered for 20 minutes, stirring frequently. Cook pasta in a large pot of boiling salted water according to package directions. Drain and place in a serving bowl. Pour hot sauce over pasta and toss until well mixed.

CHICKEN PASTA PUTTANESCA

Add 2 cups chopped cooked chicken to sauce about 5 minutes before serving.

SHRIMP OR CLAM PASTA PUTTANESCA

Add 1½ cups cooked peeled shrimp or cooked clams to sauce about 5 minutes before serving.

BAKED THREE-CHEESE RIGATONI

Servings: 4–6

You'll love this very rich, upscale version of macaroni and cheese. It can be made ahead of time, refrigerated before baking, finished in the oven and served later.

1 lb. rigatoni (or ziti, penne or any other tubular pasta)
1/4 cup (1/2 stick) butter
1/4 cup flour
4 cups milk
1 1/2 tsp. salt
1/4 tsp. ground nutmeg
1 1/2 cups shredded mozzarella cheese, divided
1 pkg. (15 oz.) ricotta cheese
1/2 cup grated Parmesan cheese

Heat oven to 350°. Spray a 9 x 13-inch baking pan with nonstick cooking spray. Cook rigatoni in a large pot of boiling salted water according to package directions; drain and keep warm. Melt butter over medium heat in a large saucepan. Add flour and whisk until smooth. Cook, stirring constantly, until mixture bubbles. Add a small amount of milk and stir until smooth.

Stir in remaining milk and cook, stirring constantly, until mixture boils. Reduce heat to low and cook for 10 minutes, stirring frequently. Remove from heat. Add salt, nutmeg, 1 cup of the mozzarella cheese, ricotta cheese and Parmesan. Stir until cheeses are melted. Add pasta and stir until very well mixed. Pour into baking pan and sprinkle with remaining ½ cup mozzarella. Bake for 45 minutes, until browned on top and bubbly.

BAKED CHEESE RIGATONI WITH SAUSAGE

Add 1 cup chopped or thinly sliced cooked smoked sausage or Italian sausage before baking.

BAKED CHEESE RIGATONI WITH TOMATOES

Add 1 cup chopped fresh tomatoes before baking.

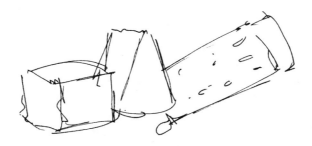

FETTUCCINE WITH TOMATO-MUSHROOM SAUCE

Although porcini mushrooms are expensive, they add a depth of flavor to this sauce that no other mushroom can replace. Substitute your favorite shape of pasta for the fettuccine.

½ oz. dried porcini mushrooms
½ cup boiling water
1 lb. fettuccine
¼ cup olive oil
1 yellow onion, chopped

2 cups chopped white mushrooms
1½ cups chopped shiitake mushrooms
2 cloves garlic, minced
1 can (28 oz.) crushed tomatoes

In a small bowl, combine porcini mushrooms and boiling water and let stand for 20 minutes. Drain mushrooms, reserving liquid. Chop mushrooms and set aside. Cook fettuccine in a large pot of boiling salted water according to package directions; drain and keep warm.

In a large saucepan, heat oil over medium-high heat. Add onion and sauté until they begin to brown. Add white mushrooms, shiitake mushrooms and garlic. Reduce heat to medium and sauté for about 5 minutes, until mushrooms are tender. Add porcini mushrooms with soaking liquid and tomatoes. Simmer uncovered for 10 minutes. Transfer fettuccine to a serving bowl and pour hot sauce over the top. Toss until combined.

FETTUCCINE WITH TOMATO-MUSHROOM AND RED WINE SAUCE

Add ½ cup red wine with porcini mushrooms and liquid.

FETTUCCINE WITH TOMATO-MUSHROOM CREAM SAUCE

After sauce has simmered for 10 minutes, remove from heat and stir in ½ cup heavy cream. Toss with hot fettuccine.

TOMATO-MUSHROOM LASAGNA

Substitute cooked lasagna sheets for the cooked fettuccine. Layer sauce over lasagna sheets in a 9 x 13-inch baking pan. Bake at 350° for 30 minutes or until hot and bubbly.

FETTUCCINE WITH SCALLOPS AND GARLIC CREAM SAUCE

Pulsing the sauce in a food processor helps to lighten its texture. Take care not to overprocess or you will wind up with whipped cream.

2 whole bulbs garlic
4 tbs. olive oil
2 tbs. butter
1 lb. sea scallops
2 cups heavy cream
1 tsp. salt
1 lb. fettuccine
1/2 cup shredded Parmesan cheese

Heat oven to 325°. Lay two sheets of aluminum foil on top of each other on a work surface. Place garlic on foil. Pour oil over garlic and tightly seal foil around garlic. Bake for about 1 hour and 15 minutes. Remove from oven and cool in foil.

In a large skillet, melt butter over medium-low heat. Add scallops and sauté until just cooked through, 8 to 10 minutes. Squeeze soft garlic pulp from papery skin into a blender container or food processor workbowl; discard skin. Add cream and salt to blender container and puree. Pour cream mixture into a small saucepan and heat over low heat until very warm. Take care that mixture does not boil.

Cook pasta in a large pot of boiling salted water according to package directions; drain. Transfer pasta to a large serving bowl. Pour cream sauce over pasta and toss to coat evenly. Sprinkle Parmesan cheese over pasta. Arrange scallops on top of pasta and serve immediately.

FETTUCCINE WITH GARLIC CREAM SAUCE

Omit butter and scallops. Serve cream sauce over the pasta.

FETTUCCINE WITH SHRIMP AND GARLIC CREAM SAUCE

Substitute shelled raw shrimp for scallops. Cook shrimp for about 8 minutes or until pink. Proceed with recipe.

SEAFOOD JAMBALAYA

Servings: 6–8

To customize this basic Creole-style stew, add sausage, ham, pork ribs, cooked bacon or any other item on hand. Add hot sauce or minced chiles for Cajun-style heat.

2 tbs. vegetable oil
1 yellow onion, chopped
1 cup chopped celery
1 cup chopped green bell pepper
2 cloves garlic, minced
1 cup long-grain rice
1 tsp. salt
1/2 tsp. crushed red pepper flakes

1 tsp. dried thyme
2 cups vegetable broth
2 bay leaves
1 pint clams
1 lb. shelled raw shrimp
1 crab, cleaned and cracked
1 can (16 oz.) tomatoes

In a stockpot, heat oil over medium heat. Add onion, celery, bell pepper and garlic and sauté until onion is translucent. Add rice, salt, red pepper flakes and thyme and stir to coat rice with oil. Add broth and bay leaves and bring mixture to a boil. Reduce heat to low, cover and simmer for about 15 minutes, until rice is barely tender.

Stir in clams, shrimp, crab and tomatoes. Cover and simmer for 10 minutes, until clams have opened and shrimp are pink. Remove bay leaves and any clams that didn't open.

SEAFOOD AND CHICKEN JAMBALAYA

Add 2 cups cubed cooked chicken with the seafood.

SEAFOOD AND PORK JAMBALAYA

Add 1 lb. baby back pork ribs with onions, celery and pepper. (Have your butcher cut ribs into 2-inch pieces.) Sauté until ribs are lightly browned. Proceed with recipe.

SEAFOOD AND SAUSAGE JAMBALAYA

Add 1 lb. cooked smoked sausage, cubed, with the seafood.

CREOLE SNAPPER

Old Bay Seasoning is most commonly used for boiling shrimp and crab. It also makes a wonderful all-purpose seasoning for both seafood and chicken. You can spice up this recipe by adding a pinch (or several pinches) of crushed red pepper flakes to the seasoning mixture.

1 tsp. Old Bay Seasoning
1 clove garlic, minced
$1/4$ tsp. salt

3 tbs. butter, melted
4 red snapper fillets, about 6 oz. each

Heat broiler. In a small bowl, combine Old Bay Seasoning, garlic, salt and butter. Stir until well mixed. Place snapper fillets on a broiler pan. Brush the tops of fish with $1/2$ of the butter mixture. Broil for 3 minutes. Baste with remaining butter mixture and broil for 3 to 5 minutes, or until fish is cooked through and flakes easily with a fork. Serve immediately.

CREOLE SOLE
Substitute sole fillets for snapper fillets.

CREOLE TURBOT
Substitute turbot fillets for snapper fillets.

TROUT WITH BALSAMIC SAUCE

Mild-tasting balsamic vinegar makes a nice sauce for an easy-to-prepare fish dish. Tailor the sauce to your personal taste by adding fresh herbs.

3 tbs. olive oil
4 medium trout fillets
1/2 cup (1 stick) butter

1 tbs. flour
1/4 cup balsamic vinegar
2 tbs. sliced green onions

Heat oil over medium-high heat in a sauté pan and sauté fillets for 2 minutes on each side, or until golden brown. In a small saucepan, melt butter over low heat. Add flour and stir until well blended. Cook mixture, stirring, for 4 minutes, taking care that it does not scorch. Remove from heat. Add balsamic vinegar and green onions and stir until well blended. Serve immediately over cooked trout.

TROUT WITH BALSAMIC BASIL SAUCE

Substitute minced fresh basil for the green onions..

TROUT WITH BALSAMIC LEMON SAUCE

Add juice and grated zest of 1 lemon with the vinegar.

GRILLED TUNA WITH CILANTRO-LIME BUTTER

Servings: 4

This easy butter-based sauce goes well with many types of grilled seafood, such as swordfish, shark or halibut. It also works well with chicken.

4 ahi tuna steaks, about 6–8 oz. each
salt and pepper to taste
½ cup (1 stick) butter

grated zest of 1 lime
1 tbs. minced fresh cilantro
¼ cup freshly squeezed lime juice

Prepare a medium-hot grill. Season tuna lightly with salt and pepper. Grill tuna steaks for 8 to 12 minutes or until firm and opaque in the center. Transfer to a serving platter. While tuna is grilling, melt butter in a small saucepan over medium heat. Add lime zest, increase heat to high and bring butter just to the boiling point. Remove from heat and stir in cilantro. Keep warm. Add lime juice to butter mixture and pour sauce over tuna steaks. Serve immediately.

GRILLED TUNA WITH PARSLEY-LEMON BUTTER

Substitute lemon zest for lime zest and minced fresh parsley for cilantro. Substitute freshly squeezed lemon juice for lime juice.

GRILLED TUNA WITH CAPER-LEMON BUTTER

Substitute lemon zest for lime zest and 4 tsp. drained capers for cilantro. Substitute freshly squeezed lemon juice for lime juice.

GRILLED CHICKEN BREASTS WITH OUTBACK SALSA

Fruit salsas lend an intriguing combination of sweet and savory flavors to grilled chicken.

4 chicken breast halves
1 cup pineapple juice
$1/4$ cup fresh lime juice, divided
6 kiwi fruit, peeled and coarsely chopped

$2/3$ cup chopped red onion
2 jalapeño peppers, seeded and minced
2 tsp. light brown sugar

In a large nonmetallic dish, combine chicken, pineapple juice and 2 tbs. of the lime juice. Cover and marinate at room temperature for 30 minutes or refrigerated for up to 4 hours. Heat a grill to medium. Grill chicken for 30 to 40 minutes until cooked through, turning occasionally. While chicken is cooking, mix together kiwi, onion, jalapeños, remaining 2 tbs. lime juice and brown sugar in a nonmetallic bowl. Spoon salsa over grilled chicken and serve immediately.

GRILLED CHICKEN BREASTS WITH VOLCANO SALSA

Substitute 2 cups chopped fresh pineapple for the kiwi. Add $1/4$ tsp. crushed red pepper flakes to the salsa.

GRILLED CHICKEN BREASTS WITH CARIBBEAN SALSA

Substitute 2 peeled, seeded, chopped papayas for the kiwi. Add $1/4$ tsp. ground allspice to the salsa.

CARIBBEAN CHICKEN

The flavorful marinade used in this dish is similar to a jerk sauce, but not quite as hot. If you would like extra fire, add half a seeded, minced habanero chile.

6 green onions, thinly sliced
1/2 yellow onion, minced
4 cloves garlic, minced
2 tbs. peeled minced fresh ginger
2 tbs. ground allspice
2 tsp. cinnamon
1 tsp. ground nutmeg
2 tsp. pepper

1/2 tsp. salt
2 tbs. dark brown sugar, packed
1 cup orange juice
3/4 cup cider vinegar
1/2 cup soy sauce
2 tbs. corn oil
8 boneless, skinless chicken breast halves

In a large nonmetallic bowl, combine green onions, yellow onion, garlic, ginger, allspice, cinnamon, nutmeg, pepper, salt, brown sugar, orange juice, vinegar, soy sauce and oil. Whisk until well blended. Add chicken and stir to coat well with marinade. Cover bowl and marinate chicken in the refrigerator for at least 8 hours.

Heat grill to medium-low. Remove chicken from marinade. Transfer marinade to a small saucepan and boil for 2 minutes; remove from heat. Grill chicken for 10 to 15 minutes, turning once, until cooked through. Baste breasts frequently with hot marinade while grilling. Serve hot.

CARIBBEAN SPARERIBS
Substitute 4 lb. pork spareribs for the chicken breasts.

CARIBBEAN PORK CHOPS
Substitute 8 thick-cut boneless pork the chops for chicken breasts.

CHICKEN AND MUSHROOMS
WITH MUSTARD-BRANDY SAUCE

This dish is a staple in country French cooking. Substitute wild mushrooms instead of white mushrooms and you will add a level of sophistication in taste and texture to your meal.

4 chicken breast halves, skin on
2 tbs. butter
2 yellow onions, chopped
8 oz. sliced fresh white mushrooms
¼ cup brandy
¼ cup grainy mustard
1 cup heavy cream

In a large stockpot over medium heat, brown chicken well, about 10 minutes per side. Remove chicken from pot and set aside. Add butter to pot. When butter is melted, add onions and sauté until just beginning to brown. Add mushrooms and sauté until juices are released and evaporate.

Remove pot from heat and add brandy. Tilt pot and carefully ignite brandy with a long match (do not do this while an overhead fan or exhaust fan is running). Shake pot until flames disperse. Add mustard and cream and stir well. Return chicken breasts to pot, cover and simmer over low heat for 15 minutes, or until chicken is cooked through. Take care that sauce does not boil.

CHICKEN WITH MUSTARD-BRANDY SAUCE
Omit mushrooms.

CHICKEN WITH MUSTARD-SHERRY SAUCE
Omit mushrooms. Substitute dry sherry for brandy.

CHICKEN AND MUSHROOMS WITH BRANDY SAUCE
Omit mustard.

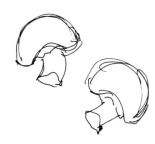

STIR-FRIED CHICKEN WITH TWO ONIONS

This recipe combines the flavors of a Chinese-style chicken stir-fry and French onion soup. The result is an easily prepared savory treat. Try adding broccoli or sliced red peppers for some color and crunch. Serve over steamed rice or pasta.

2 tbs. plus 1 tsp. cornstarch, divided
1/4 cup plus 1 tbs. dry sherry, divided
3 boneless, skinless chicken breast halves, sliced thinly
1 tbs. vegetable oil
2 yellow onions, sliced
1 tbs. Worcestershire sauce
3/4 cup chicken broth
6 green onions, cut into 1-inch slices

In a medium bowl, stir together 1 tsp. of the cornstarch and 1 tbs. of the sherry. Add chicken and toss to coat evenly. Let stand for 15 minutes.

Drain excess liquid from chicken. Heat a large skillet or wok over high heat. Add oil. Add chicken and stir-fry until chicken turns opaque. Add yellow onions and stir-fry just until onions soften and turn translucent. In a small bowl, whisk together remaining ¼ cup sherry, Worcestershire sauce, broth and remaining 2 tbs. cornstarch until smooth. Pour mixture over chicken and onions in pan, stirring constantly. Add green onions and stir-fry until sauce comes to a boil and thickens. Serve immediately.

STIR-FRIED BEEF WITH TWO ONIONS
Substitute 2 cups sliced beef for chicken.

STIR-FRIED CHICKEN WITH WINE AND TWO ONIONS
Substitute white wine for sherry.

STIR-FRIED CHICKEN WITH YELLOW ONIONS
Omit green onions.

BRAISED CHICKEN
WITH ARTICHOKES AND TOMATOES

Servings: 6–8

This is a traditional Northern Italian presentation of a chicken stew. Try it served over polenta or tiny pasta to soak up the delicious sauce.

1 tbs. olive oil
1 chicken, 3 lb., cut into serving pieces
1 yellow onion, sliced
2 cloves garlic, minced

2 cups artichoke hearts
1 cup dry white wine
2 cups chopped tomatoes
$1/2$ tsp. salt

In a large skillet, heat oil over medium heat. Add chicken pieces and brown on all sides. Remove chicken from skillet and set aside. Add onion and garlic and sauté until they begin to brown. Add artichoke hearts, wine, tomatoes and salt and bring mixture to a boil. Add chicken pieces. Cover skillet, reduce heat to low and simmer for 15 minutes, until chicken is cooked through. Serve immediately.

BRAISED CHICKEN BREASTS WITH ARTICHOKES AND TOMATOES
Substitute 4 large chicken breast halves for the chicken pieces.

BRAISED CHICKEN WITH WHITE WINE AND ARTICHOKES
Omit tomatoes. Add 1 cup chicken broth along with the artichokes.

ROASTED CHICKEN WITH FRESH SAGE

Fresh sage and dry white wine pair well with a recipe for a classic roast chicken dinner.

1 tbs. finely minced fresh sage
½ cup (1 stick) butter, softened
½ tsp. salt

1 roasting chicken, cut into pieces
½ cup dry white wine

Heat oven to 375°. In a small bowl, blend together sage, butter and salt. Rub butter mixture over the surface of all chicken pieces. Arrange chicken in a 9 x 13-inch baking pan. Bake for 30 minutes. Pour wine over chicken and bake for 10 additional minutes, until chicken is cooked through. Transfer chicken to a platter. Remove fat from the surface of pan juices and strain juices into a bowl for serving.

ROASTED CHICKEN WITH FRESH SAGE AND LEMON

Add juice of 1 lemon with wine.

ROASTED CHICKEN WITH FRESH THYME

Substitute minced fresh thyme for the sage.

ROASTED CHICKEN WITH CHERVIL

Substitute minced fresh chervil for the sage.

ROASTED CHICKEN WITH RICE-WALNUT STUFFING

Servings: 6–8

Nuts and rice are a simple yet rich-tasting combination. Here they are used as a stuffing for an easy-to-prepare roasted chicken.

2 tbs. butter
1 yellow onion, chopped
3/4 cup chopped walnuts
1/4 tsp. ground thyme
1/4 tsp. ground sage
1 tsp. salt

2 1/2 cups cooked white rice
1 roasting chicken, 5 lb.
2 tbs. walnut oil
5–6 cups chicken broth
1/4 cup flour

Heat oven to 325°. In a medium skillet, melt butter over medium heat. Add onion and sauté until translucent. Add walnuts and sauté until onion begins to brown and walnuts are toasted. Remove skillet from heat and stir in thyme, sage, salt and rice. Set aside. Remove giblets from chicken and rinse surface and cavity with cold running water. Drain well and pat skin dry. Spoon stuffing loosely into body cavity and tie legs together with kitchen string to hold stuffing inside. Rub outside of chicken with walnut oil. Place chicken in a roasting pan. Roast for 2 1/2 to 3 hours, or until a thermometer reads 180° to 185° when inserted into thickest part of thigh. Baste chicken frequently with broth during roasting.

Transfer chicken to a serving platter. Add chicken broth to pan drippings, if necessary, to measure 4 cups. Pour mixture into a medium saucepan. Sprinkle flour over mixture and mix well with a wire whisk. Bring gravy to a boil over high heat, stirring constantly. Reduce heat to low and simmer for 5 minutes, stirring frequently, until thickened. Strain gravy through a sieve and transfer to a gravy boat. Remove stuffing from chicken cavity and place on a serving plate. Carve chicken into serving pieces and serve with stuffing and gravy.

ROASTED CHICKEN WITH RICE-HAZELNUT STUFFING

Substitute chopped hazelnuts for the walnuts; substitute vegetable oil for the walnut oil.

ROASTED CHICKEN WITH RICE-CASHEW STUFFING

Substitute cashew pieces for the walnuts; substitute vegetable oil for the walnut oil.

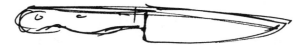

CHIPOTLE PORK STEW

Servings: 6

Chipotle peppers, otherwise known as smoked jalapeños, add fire and a subtle smoky flavor to this pork dish. Always rehydrate the chipotles before attempting to remove the seeds and ribs. Look for dried chipotle peppers in Latin American markets or specialty food stores. Serve this stew over steamed rice, or with crusty bread to soak up the sauce.

/2 cup boiling water
3 dried chipotle peppers
1 tbs. vegetable oil
2 lb. boneless pork, cubed
¹1 can (15 oz.) peeled tomatoes
2 cups chicken broth
1 yellow onion, chopped
2 cloves garlic, minced
1/2 tsp. ground cumin
1/2 tsp. salt

Combine boiling water and chipotles in a small bowl and let stand for 15 minutes . Drain peppers, reserving liquid, and remove seeds and ribs. Coarsely chop peppers. Set aside.

In a stockpot, heat oil over medium-high heat. Add pork and sauté until pork begins to brown, about 15 minutes. Add reserved chipotle liquid, chipotles, tomatoes, broth, onion, garlic, cumin and salt to pot with pork. Bring mixture to a boil over high heat. Reduce heat to low and simmer uncovered for 2 hours or until pork is fork-tender and sauce is thickened and reduced.

CHIPOTLE PORK AND VEGETABLE STEW

Simmer stew for 1 hour. Add 1½ cups chopped carrots and 1½ cups cubed potatoes and simmer 1 hour longer, until pork and vegetables are tender and sauce is thickened.

SAUCY CHIPOTLE PORK RIBS

Substitute 4 lb. pork spareribs for the boneless pork.

HONEY-MUSTARD PORK TENDERLOIN

Servings: 4

You can also prepare this dish by grilling the pork and then basting with the honey mustard sauce in the final minutes of grilling. The smoky flavor of grilling accents the sweetness of the honey. When basting any meat with a sweet sauce, make sure to keep the meat over very low or indirect heat to prevent burning.

2 pork tenderloins, 1 lb. each
1/2 cup apple juice, divided

1/2 cup grainy mustard
1/2 cup honey

Heat oven to 325°. Spray a 9 x 13-inch baking pan with nonstick cooking spray. Cut tenderloins into 8 thick slices and place in a shallow dish with 1/3 cup of the apple juice. Marinate at room temperature for 30 minutes, turning once. In a small bowl, combine mustard, honey and remaining apple juice. Remove pork from marinade and pat dry. Rub mustard mixture over pork slices and place in prepared pan. Cover dish tightly with foil. Bake pork for 30 minutes or until cooked through.

MAPLE-MUSTARD PORK TENDERLOIN
Substitute 1/2 cup maple syrup for the honey.

ORANGE-MUSTARD PORK TENDERLOIN
Substitute freshly squeezed orange juice for the apple juice.

PORK CHOPS WITH ORANGE-BOURBON SAUCE

Servings: 6–8

This sauce dresses up ordinary old pork chops. If the month has been profitable, consider purchasing a fine bottle of bourbon. Blanton's, Baker's, or Maker's Mark are all good choices.

1 tbs. vegetable oil
4 thick-cut boneless pork chops
½ cup bourbon

1 cup orange juice
2 tbs. honey
1 lb. sweet potatoes, peeled and thickly sliced

In a large skillet, heat oil over medium heat. Add pork chops and brown lightly on both sides, about 10 minutes per side. Remove from pan and set aside. Remove pan from heat and pour out any excess fat. Off heat, add bourbon to skillet. Tilt skillet and carefully ignite bourbon using a long match (do not attempt this while an overhead fan or exhaust fan is running). Shake skillet until flames disperse. Add orange juice and honey to skillet and bring to a boil over high heat. Reduce heat to low and add potatoes. Place pork chops on top of potatoes. Cover and simmer until potatoes are tender and pork is cooked through, about 20 minutes. Serve immediately.

PORK CHOPS WITH ORANGE SAUCE
Omit bourbon.

PORK CHOPS AND APPLES WITH ORANGE-BOURBON SAUCE
Arrange 2 sliced Granny Smith apples on top of pork chops before simmering in covered skillet.

ITALIAN BEEF STEW

For a traditional Italian meal, spoon this stew over cooked polenta. It is even better the next day!

2 tbs. olive oil
1 yellow onion, chopped
2 cloves garlic, minced
2 lb. cubed beef stew meat
1/2 cup chopped fresh Italian parsley
1 cup dry red wine

4 cups peeled coarsely chopped Roma
   tomatoes
2 cups beef broth
1/4 tsp. pepper
1/4 tsp. cinnamon
1/2 tsp. salt

In a stockpot, heat olive oil over medium-high heat. Add onion and garlic and sauté until onion is translucent. Add beef and increase heat to high. Sauté until beef just begins to brown. Add parsley, wine, tomatoes, broth, pepper, cinnamon and salt and bring mixture to a boil over high heat. Reduce heat to low and simmer uncovered for 2 hours or until beef is fork-tender.

ITALIAN BEEF STEW WITH VEGETABLES

About 45 minutes before serving, add 2 medium zucchini (thickly sliced), 2 carrots (thickly sliced) and 1 1/2 cups halved fresh green beans.

HERBED ITALIAN BEEF STEW

Substitute 1 tsp. dried oregano and 1 tsp. dried basil for the cinnamon.

GRILLED FILET MIGNON WITH CHILE BUTTER

Servings: 4

Good cuts of beef seldom need more than a touch of sauce to accent their flavors. The beef is marinated with red wine and topped with a touch of rich-flavored butter.

1 cup dry red wine
2 tbs. balsamic vinegar
1/2 tsp. pepper
1 clove garlic, finely minced
4 filet mignon steaks

1/4 cup (1/2 stick) butter, softened
1/8 tsp. crushed red pepper flakes
1/4 tsp. ground cumin
1/8 tsp. cayenne pepper

In a shallow nonmetallic dish, combine wine, vinegar, pepper and garlic. Add steaks, cover and marinate for 30 minutes at room temperature or up to 4 hours in the refrigerator. Combine butter, pepper flakes, cumin and cayenne in a small bowl. Mix until well blended and set aside. Broil or grill steaks to desired doneness. Place 1 tbs. chile butter on each steak and serve immediately.

GRILLED FILET MIGNON WITH BLUE CHEESE BUTTER

Omit pepper flakes, cumin and cayenne. Add 1/4 cup crumbled blue cheese to the butter.

FILET MIGNON WITH GARLIC HERB BUTTER

Omit pepper flakes, cumin and cayenne. Add 1 clove minced garlic and 1 tsp. minced chives to the butter.

BEEF ROAST WITH WINTER VEGETABLES

Changing vegetables in recipes can give you dramatically different results. Here, a beef roast can be presented at any time of the year, depending on the vegetables that are available.

1 tbs. vegetable oil
1 rib-eye roast, 4 lb.
3-3½ cups beef broth, divided
5 black peppercorns
1 bay leaf
1 clove garlic, chopped

1 tsp. salt
8 small potatoes, cut in half
8 carrots, cut in half
2 yellow onions, quartered
4 turnips, quartered
¼ cup flour

Heat oven to 325°. In a large Dutch oven, heat oil over medium-high heat. Add beef roast and brown on all sides. Add 1 cup of the broth, peppercorns, bay leaf, garlic and salt to pot. Bring mixture to a boil. Cover pot, transfer to oven and bake for 2½ hours. Add potatoes, carrots, onions and turnips to pot and bake covered for an additional 45 to 60 minutes or until beef and vegetables are tender. Transfer beef and vegetables to a serving platter; keep warm while preparing gravy.

Skim excess fat from pan juices. Add beef broth, if necessary, to pan juices to equal 2 cups. Pour into a small saucepan. In a small bowl, whisk together flour and ½ cup of the broth until smooth. Gradually stir flour mixture into pan juices and mix well until smooth.

Bring gravy to a boil over medium heat. Boil for 1 minute, stirring constantly. Serve with beef and vegetables.

BEEF ROAST WITH SPRING VEGETABLES

Omit potatoes, carrots, onions and turnips. Bake roast for 3 hours. Add ½ lb. trimmed whole baby zucchini or other baby squash, ½ lb. trimmed whole baby carrots and 8 green onions, quartered. Cover and bake for an additional ½ hour.

BEEF ROAST WITH AUTUMN VEGETABLES

Substitute 6 halved Yukon Gold potatoes, 1 lb. 2-inch chunks butternut squash and 2 quartered yellow bell peppers for the potatoes, carrots, onions and turnips.

GARLIC BEEF PROVENÇAL WITH LEEKS

You will love the way your home smells as this beef roasts in your oven. Serve it with your favorite roasted potatoes and a smooth red wine.

1 tbs. olive oil
1 beef roast, 3–4 lb.
6 cloves garlic, sliced
2 cups sliced leeks
1½ tsp. fresh thyme
2 bay leaves
1 cup dry red wine
1 tsp. salt
½ tsp. pepper
¼ cup beef broth
3 tbs. flour

Heat oven to 325°. In a large Dutch oven, heat oil over medium heat. Add beef roast and brown evenly on all sides. Add garlic, leeks, thyme, bay leaves, wine, salt and pepper. Cover and bake for 2½ to 3 hours or until meat is fork-tender.

Transfer meat to a cutting board and let stand for 10 minutes. Strain pan juices, reserving leeks and garlic, and discarding bay leaves. Pour juices into a small saucepan. Bring to a boil over medium-high heat. Mix together broth and flour until smooth. Slowly stir flour mixture into boiling juices, stirring constantly. Reduce heat to medium and cook for 5 minutes, stirring constantly. Return leeks and garlic to thickened sauce. Slice beef against the grain and place on a serving platter. Pour leek sauce over sliced beef and serve immediately.

GARLIC BEEF PROVENÇAL
Omit leeks.

GARLIC BEEF PROVENÇAL WITH ONIONS
Substitute 1 cup thinly sliced yellow onion for the leeks.

BEEF PROVENÇAL
Reduce garlic to 1 clove.

MEXICAN FLANK STEAK

Servings: 4

Flank steak absorbs flavors well. With a simple rub, this grilled steak becomes very juicy and flavorful.

juice of 2 limes
2 tsp. ground cumin
1/2 tsp. cayenne pepper
1/2 tsp. pepper

2 tbs. sliced green onions
1 clove garlic, minced
1 lb. flank steak

In a small bowl, combine lime juice, cumin, cayenne, black pepper, green onions and garlic until mixture forms a thin paste. Rub paste over both sides of flank steak. Refrigerate, covered, for 4 hours. Prepare a medium-hot grill. Grill meat to desired doneness. To serve, slice against the grain and arrange on a platter.

MEXICAN FLANK STEAK WITH PEPPERS

Core seed and quarter 1 green and 1 red bell pepper. Grill peppers with steak until tender-crisp. Serve grilled peppers with sliced flank steak.

MEXICAN FLANK STEAK WITH SMOKY ONIONS

Slice 2 yellow onions into 4 thick rings each. Grill onions with steak until charred on each side. Serve grilled onions with sliced flank steak.

PAN-SEARED FILET MIGNON WITH BRIE SAUCE

This is the recipe to go off your diet for! Tender beef needs only a simple Brie sauce to show off its flavors. The variations let you experiment with other rich cheeses.

¼ cup (½ stick) butter
4 filet mignon steaks, 1½ inches thick
½ cup heavy cream

½ cup chopped Brie cheese, rind removed
¼ tsp. pepper

In a large skillet, heat butter over medium-high heat. Add steaks and cook until evenly browned, about 2 minutes on each side for rare or about 3 minutes on each side for medium. Transfer steaks to a serving platter and keep warm. Reduce heat to medium-low and add cream, Brie and pepper to skillet. Cook, stirring constantly, until Brie is melted and sauce is hot; make sure that mixture does not boil. Spoon hot sauce over steaks and serve immediately.

PAN-SEARED FILET MIGNON WITH HERBED BRIE SAUCE
Substitute herbed Brie cheese for the regular Brie.

PAN-SEARED FILET MIGNON WITH PEPPERCORN BRIE SAUCE
Substitute peppercorn Brie cheese for the regular Brie.

PAN-SEARED FILET MIGNON WITH GORGONZOLA SAUCE
Substitute crumbled Gorgonzola for the Brie.

DESSERTS

NUTTY BISCOTTI

These biscotti are not quite as hard and dry as those you can purchase and are still delicious when you dip them into your espresso.

²⁄₃ cup butter, softened	4¹⁄₂ cups flour
1¹⁄₂ cups sugar	1 tbs. baking powder
4 eggs	¹⁄₂ tsp. salt
1 tbs. vanilla extract	1 cup chopped pecans

Heat oven to 325°. Grease a cookie sheet. In a large bowl, beat butter and sugar with a mixer until light and fluffy. Beat in eggs and vanilla until well mixed. Add flour, baking powder, salt and pecans and mix until dough is well blended. Divide dough into 4 equal portions. Shape each portion into a log about 12 inches long. Place logs on prepared cookie sheet about 2 inches apart. Bake for 25 to 30 minutes or until logs are just beginning to brown. Cool logs for 10 minutes. Cut into diagonal slices ¹⁄₂-inch thick. Lay slices flat on cookie sheet. Bake slices for 5 minutes. Turn and bake until golden, about 5 more minutes. Cool on a rack.

PINE NUT, WALNUT OR ALMOND BISCOTTI

Substitute pine nuts, chopped walnuts or slivered almonds for the pecans.

BISCOTTI CRUMBLES

Think of these as dessert croutons. They can top your favorite ice cream or gelato or be sprinkled over fresh fruit. The biscotti should be crumbled into pieces the size of small croutons.

¼ cup (½ stick) butter
2 cups crumbled plain biscotti

¼ tsp. cinnamon

In a medium saucepan, heat butter over medium heat until melted. Add crumbled biscotti and cinnamon and stir until evenly coated. Cook, stirring, until biscotti are golden brown, about 10 minutes. Cool mixture and store in a covered container in the refrigerator until ready to use.

OATMEAL CRUMBLES
Substitute crumbled plain oatmeal cookies for biscotti.

SHORTBREAD CRUMBLES
Substitute crumbled plain Scotch shortbread or plain sugar cookies for biscotti.

NUTTY BISCOTTI CRUMBLES
Substitute crumbled biscotti with nuts for plain biscotti.

CHOCOLATE CHIP COOKIES

There are many recipes for chocolate chip cookies and each version is a bit different. This recipe yields a soft, chewy cookie with lots of options for personalized variations.

1 cup (2 sticks) butter, softened
1 cup light brown sugar, packed
1/2 cup granulated sugar
2 eggs
2 tsp. vanilla extract

2 3/4 cups flour
1 tsp. baking soda
1 tsp. salt
1 pkg. (12 oz.) semisweet chocolate chips

Heat oven to 325°. In a large bowl, beat butter, brown sugar and granulated sugar until light and fluffy. Beat in eggs and vanilla. Add flour, baking soda and salt and mix well. Stir in chocolate chips. Drop dough by rounded tablespoonfuls onto an ungreased cookie sheet. Bake about 12 minutes until golden. Cool on pan for 5 minutes. Transfer cookies to a rack to cool completely.

CHOCOLATE CHIP-WALNUT COOKIES

Stir in 1 cup chopped walnuts when adding chocolate chips.

WHITE CHOCOLATE-MACADAMIA COOKIES

Substitute white chocolate chips for chocolate chips and add 1 cup chopped macadamia nuts.

OATMEAL RAISIN COOKIES

Soft and chewy with lots of raisins, these cookies are destined to become one of your favorites. They are very easy to modify by using different dried fruits and nuts.

1 cup (2 sticks) butter, softened
1 cup light brown sugar, packed
½ cup granulated sugar
2 eggs
1 tsp. vanilla extract

2 cups quick cooking oats
1½ cups flour
1 tsp. baking soda
1 tsp. salt
1 cup raisins

Heat oven to 350°. In a large bowl, beat butter, brown sugar and granulated sugar until light and fluffy. Beat in eggs and vanilla. Add oats, flour, baking soda and salt and mix well. Stir in raisins. Drop dough by rounded tablespoonfuls onto an ungreased cookie sheet. Bake about 12 minutes until golden. Cool on pan for 5 minutes. Transfer cookies to a rack to cool completely.

OATMEAL RAISIN WALNUT COOKIES

Add 1 cup chopped walnuts when adding raisins.

FRUITY OATMEAL COOKIES

Substitute sweetened dried cranberries or chopped dried apples, apricots or pears for raisins.

LEMON COOKIES

These little cookies have a big rich taste. They're wonderful served with tea or evening coffee.

1 cup (2 sticks) butter, softened
8 oz. cream cheese, softened
2 cups sugar

1 tsp. lemon extract
1 tsp. grated fresh lemon zest
2 cups flour

In a large bowl, beat butter and cream cheese with a mixer until light and fluffy. Add sugar, lemon extract and zest and mix until creamy. Add flour and mix well. Form dough into a ball. Cover with plastic wrap and refrigerate for at least 2 hours.

Heat oven to 350°. Roll dough between hands to form ping pong-sized balls. Place balls about 2 inches apart on an ungreased cookie sheet. Bake 12 to 14 minutes until edges just begin to brown. Transfer cookies to a wire rack to cool completely. Store in an airtight container.

LEMON COCONUT COOKIES
Add ½ cup flaked coconut to dough.

CITRUS CONFETTI COOKIES
Substitute ¾ tsp. grated fresh orange zest and ½ tsp. grated fresh lime zest for the lemon zest.

VANILLA CREAM CHEESE COOKIES
Substitute 2 tsp. vanilla extract for the lemon extract and lemon zest.

BLACKBERRY BARS

Although these are cookies, they are healthy enough to be served as breakfast bars. The wheat germ and oats add a delectable crunch. Store uneaten bars in an airtight container.

2½ cups fresh or frozen blackberries
1 tbs. cornstarch
½ cup granulated sugar
¾ cup (1½ sticks) butter, softened
1 cup brown sugar, packed
3 eggs

1½ cups whole wheat flour
¾ cup wheat germ, toasted
1½ tsp. baking soda
¾ tsp. salt
2¼ cups quick cooking oats

Heat oven to 375°. Spray the bottom and sides of a 9 x 13-inch baking pan with nonstick cooking spray. In a medium saucepan, stir together blackberries, cornstarch and granulated sugar. Cook over medium heat, stirring frequently, until berries collapse and juices coat the back of a spoon. Cool and set aside.

With a mixer, beat butter and brown sugar until light and creamy. Add eggs and beat for 1 minute. In another bowl, stir together flour, wheat germ, baking soda, salt and oats. Add flour mixture to butter mixture and mix well. Divide dough in half. Press half evenly into bottom of prepared pan. Pour berry mixture over the top and gently spread to within 1/4 inch of the edge. Crumble remaining half of dough over berry mixture. Bake about 20 minutes until edges are lightly browned. Cool in pan and cut into 3-x3-inch bars.

RASPBERRY BARS

Substitute fresh or frozen raspberries for the blackberries.

STRAWBERRY BARS

Substitute fresh or frozen strawberries for the blackberries.

MIXED BERRY COBBLER

Combining different fruits into a cobbler complements fruit flavors; plus it's easy and delicious.

2 cups fresh blackberries
2 cups fresh raspberries
1 cup fresh blueberries
½ cup plus 1 tbs. sugar, divided
1 tbs. cornstarch

1 cup flour
1½ tsp. baking powder
½ tsp. salt
3 tbs. butter
½ cup milk

Heat oven to 375°. In a large bowl, combine blackberries, raspberries, blueberries, ½ cup of the sugar and cornstarch and toss gently until mixed. Pour into an 8 x 8-inch baking pan. In a medium bowl, combine flour, remaining 1 tbs. sugar, baking powder and salt. With a pastry blender or two knives, cut in butter until mixture resembles fine crumbs. Stir in milk and mix just until mixture is moistened. Drop dough over berry mixture in pan, distributing evenly. Bake 30 to 35 minutes until topping is golden brown and berry mixture is bubbling. Serve warm.

ORANGE-SCENTED BERRY COBBLER
Omit blueberries. Increase blackberries to 3 cups. Add 1 tbs. grated orange zest to fruit mixture.

PEACH-BERRY COBBLER
Substitute 2 cups peeled sliced fresh peaches for the blueberries.

SPICED BLACKBERRY PIE

Frozen blackberries are readily available, which make this pie perfect for summer or winter. The spicy flavors make this pie a great finish to a holiday meal.

dough for one 9-inch double-crust pie
6 cups fresh blackberries or frozen
   blackberries, thawed
¾ cup sugar

¼ cup flour
¾ tsp. cinnamon
¼ tsp. ground nutmeg
¼ tsp. ground allspice

Heat oven to 425°. Line a 9-inch pie pan with half of the piecrust dough. Reserve remaining dough. In a large bowl, mix together berries, sugar, flour, cinnamon, nutmeg and allspice. Pour berry mixture into crust. Roll out reserved dough slightly and position on top of filling, crimping edges to seal. Slit top to allow steam to escape. Bake for about 45 minutes until golden brown. If crust begins to brown too quickly, cover pie with a sheet of aluminum foil while baking.

SPICED APPLE-BLACKBERRY PIE

Reduce blackberries to 3 cups. Toss 3 cups sliced, peeled Pippin apples with berries.

BLACKBERRY PIE

Omit any or all of the spices.

VANILLA ALMOND SNOW PIE

Here's a festive "snowy" take on a traditional mud pie.

3 eggs
1 cup sugar
2 cups milk
1 tsp. vanilla extract

1 tsp. almond extract
½ cup sliced almonds
2 cups heavy cream
1 prepared vanilla wafer piecrust

In a medium saucepan, beat eggs and sugar. Add milk and mix well. Cook mixture over medium heat, stirring constantly, until it thickens and coats the back of a spoon, about 15 minutes. Transfer to a covered container and refrigerate for at least 4 hours or until very cold. Stir in vanilla, almond extract, almonds and cream until well mixed. Transfer to an ice cream maker and freeze according to manufacturer's directions. Mound ice cream in piecrust, cover with plastic wrap and freeze until firm, about 3 hours. Let pie stand at room temperature for 10 minutes before cutting.

VANILLA SNOW PIE

Omit almond extract and almonds. Increase vanilla extract to 1 tbs.

PEPPERMINT SNOW PIE

Substitute 1 tsp. peppermint extract and ½ cup crushed peppermint candies for the almond extract and almonds.

MOCHA MUD PIE

Mud pie is even more of a treat when you make it with homemade ice cream. Top it with your favorite chocolate sauce and whipped cream.

3 eggs	1 tbs. instant coffee powder
1 cup sugar	1 tsp. vanilla extract
2 cups milk	2 cups heavy cream
2 squares (1 oz. each) unsweetened chocolate	1 prepared chocolate wafer piecrust

In a medium saucepan, beat eggs and sugar. Add milk and mix well. Cook mixture over medium heat, stirring constantly, until it thickens and coats the back of a spoon, about 15 minutes. Melt chocolate in a microwave or in a saucepan over low heat. Add to egg mixture and mix well. Add instant coffee and stir until coffee is dissolved and mixture is smooth. Transfer to a covered container and refrigerate for at least 4 hours or until very cold. Stir in vanilla and cream. Transfer mixture to an ice cream maker and freeze according to manufacturer's directions. Mound ice cream in piecrust. Cover with plastic wrap and freeze until firm, about 3 hours. Let pie stand at room temperature for 10 minutes before cutting.

CHOCOLATE MUD PIE
　　Omit coffee.

CAPPUCCINO MUD PIE
　　Omit chocolate. Increase coffee to 1/4 cup.

WHITE CHOCOLATE SIN

White chocolate plus butter and sugar equals pure sin. This is a very sweet and rich dessert; try serving it with a tart berry sauce to offset the sweetness.

1 cup white chocolate chips
½ cup (1 stick) butter
3 eggs
1 cup sugar

½ tsp. vanilla extract
¾ cup flour
fresh raspberries or blackberries, optional

Heat oven to 350°. Spray the bottom and sides of a 9-inch springform pan with nonstick cooking spray. In a small saucepan, combine white chocolate and butter. Cook over low heat, stirring, until mixture is melted and smooth. In a large bowl, beat eggs, sugar and vanilla with a mixer on high speed for 2 minutes. Reduce speed to low and slowly pour in chocolate mixture. Mix until thoroughly blended. Stir in flour with a spoon until just incorporated. Pour batter into prepared pan. Bake about 35 minutes until the center is firm to the touch and the top is golden. Cool on a wire rack. Serve at room temperature with berries, if desired.

MILK OR BITTERSWEET CHOCOLATE SIN
Substitute milk or bittersweet chocolate chips for white chocolate chips.

FRESH APPLE WALNUT CAKE

Servings: 8

This recipe, at least three generations old, came from Italy to America with my grandmother. Do not rely on the "toothpick test" to test this cake's doneness, as it is very moist and dense.

1 cup sugar
1 egg, beaten
$\frac{1}{2}$ cup (1 stick) butter, melted
1 cup flour
1 tsp. baking soda

$\frac{1}{2}$ tsp. cinnamon
$\frac{1}{4}$ tsp. salt
2 cups peeled, coarsely chopped Granny
    Smith apples
$\frac{1}{2}$ cup chopped walnuts

Heat oven to 375°. Spray an 8x8-inch baking pan with nonstick cooking spray. In a large bowl, beat together sugar, egg and butter with a mixer until smooth. In a small bowl, sift together flour, baking soda, cinnamon and salt. Add flour mixture to egg mixture and stir just until mixed. Add apples and walnuts and stir just until mixed. Transfer batter to prepared pan. Bake for 30 minutes. Cool in pan and serve warm or cold.

APPLE SPICE CAKE

Omit walnuts. Add $\frac{1}{2}$ tsp. ground allspice and $\frac{1}{4}$ tsp. ground nutmeg to flour.

APPLE CAKE

Omit walnuts.

CALIFORNIA STRAWBERRY SHORTCAKES

Real shortcakes are a type of biscuit, not at all like the sponge cakes available at the super-market. The biscuit absorbs some of the juices and creates a nice contrast to the ripe berries.

$1/4$ cup plus 2 tbs. sugar, divided
2 cups plus 2 tbs. flour
2 tsp. baking powder
1 tsp. salt
5 tbs. vegetable shortening

grated zest of 1 orange
$3/4$ cup milk
2 cups sliced fresh strawberries
1 tbs. Grand Marnier, optional
whipped cream for garnish

Heat oven to 425°. In a large bowl, sift 2 tbs. of the sugar, flour, baking powder and salt. With a pastry blender or two knives, cut in shortening until mixture resembles coarse crumbs. Add orange zest and milk. Stir just until mixture forms a soft dough that leaves the sides of bowl. Transfer dough to a lightly floured surface. Knead dough 6 or 8 times. Roll out dough to $3/4$-inch thick. With a floured 2-inch biscuit cutter, cut dough and place on an ungreased cookie sheet. Bake 12 to 18 minutes until light golden brown. Cool on a rack.

In a small bowl, mix strawberries, sugar and Grand Marnier (if using), and let stand for 30 minutes. Slice shortcakes in half and place bottom halves on dessert plates. Top each shortcake half with a spoonful of strawberry mixture and whipped cream. Place remaining shortcake half on top. Serve immediately.

LEMON AND BERRY SHORTCAKES

Substitute grated lemon zest for the orange zest. Omit Grand Marnier. Substitute 2 cups fresh or frozen blackberries for the strawberries.

MIXED BERRY SHORTCAKES

Reduce strawberries to 1 cup. Add ½ cup fresh blueberries and ½ cup blackberries or raspberries.

BITTERSWEET CHOCOLATE CAKE

This is a cake that everyone loves. If desired, you can frost this cake with cream cheese frosting or your favorite chocolate frosting flavored with 1 tsp. rum extract.

½ cup (1 stick) butter, softened
1¼ cups sugar
3 eggs
¾ cup milk
1 tsp. vanilla extract

½ cup unsweetened cocoa powder
1¼ cups cake flour
½ tsp. salt
½ tsp. baking soda

Heat oven to 350°. Butter and flour the bottom and sides of a 9 x 13-inch baking pan. In a large bowl, beat butter and sugar with a mixer until light and fluffy. Add eggs and beat until light yellow in color. Beat in milk and vanilla. In a small bowl, sift together cocoa powder, flour, salt and baking soda. Add flour mixture to egg mixture and mix just until incorporated. Pour batter into prepared pan. Bake for 20 to 25 minutes or until a toothpick inserted into the center comes out clean.

BITTERSWEET CHOCOLATE LAYER CAKE

Pour batter into two 9-inch round cake pans. Bake for 18 to 23 minutes.

DARK CHOCOLATE CAKE

Substitute 1¼ cups light brown sugar, packed, for the granulated sugar.

CHOCOLATE WALNUT TORTE

Servings: 8–10

This impressive dessert is rich and satisfying. It is also quick to assemble and virtually fool-proof. Changing the types of chocolate and nuts gives you quite a few options for personalizing the recipe. You can also use almond, peppermint or orange extract in place of vanilla.

½ cup (1 stick) butter
10 oz. bittersweet chocolate
4 eggs
¾ cup sugar
1 tsp. vanilla extract

¾ cup flour
½ tsp. baking powder
1 cup chopped walnuts
Raspberry Sauce, page 147, optional

Heat oven to 350°. Spray the bottom and sides of a 9-inch springform pan with nonstick cooking spray. In a medium saucepan, combine butter and chocolate. Melt over low heat, stirring frequently, until smooth. In a large bowl, beat eggs with a mixer until light yellow in color. Beat in sugar and vanilla. Stir in chocolate mixture. Beat in flour, baking powder and walnuts. Transfer batter to prepared pan. Bake for 30 to 35 minutes, or until a toothpick inserted into the center comes out clean. Cool cake in pan. Serve with *Raspberry Sauce,* if desired.

CHOCOLATE ALMOND OR HAZELNUT TORTE
Substitute slivered almonds or chopped hazelnuts for the walnuts.

BUTTER CAKE

Here is a basic recipe for quick butter cake, which you can tailor to your personal taste. It goes together quickly, using ingredients you probably already have in your refrigerator and pantry.

1½ cups flour
2 tsp. baking powder
½ tsp. salt
½ cup sugar

½ cup (1 stick) butter
½ cup milk
1 egg, beaten

Heat oven to 400°. Spray an 8 x 8-inch baking pan with nonstick cooking spray. In a medium bowl, mix together flour, baking powder, salt and sugar. In a small saucepan, melt butter over low heat. Cool for 5 minutes.; beat in milk and egg. Pour butter mixture into flour mixture and stir until well mixed. Transfer batter to prepared pan. Bake for 20 to 25 minutes, or until a toothpick inserted into center of cake comes out clean.

CHOCOLATE CHIP BUTTER CAKE

Stir 1 cup semisweet, milk or white chocolate chips into batter.

CHOCOLATE CHIP-NUT BUTTER CAKE

Stir ¾ cup semisweet, milk or white chocolate chips chocolate chips and ½ cup chopped walnuts, pecans or almonds into batter.

BANANA BREAD PUDDING

In this recipe, bananas are added to a basic bread pudding for a very moist and flavorful version of a family favorite.

3 ripe bananas, mashed
4 cups white bread pieces
4 eggs
3 cups milk

$\frac{1}{3}$ cup sugar
1 tsp. salt
2 tsp. vanilla extract

Heat oven to 350°. Spray the bottom and sides of a 9-x-13-inch baking pan with nonstick cooking spray. In a large bowl, mix together mashed bananas and bread pieces. In a small bowl, beat together eggs, milk, sugar, salt and vanilla. Pour milk mixture over bread and bananas and stir to mix well. Transfer bread mixture to prepared pan. Bake 35 to 45 minutes until firm and just beginning to brown on top. Cool for 10 minutes before serving.

CHOCOLATE CHIP BANANA BREAD PUDDING

Add $\frac{1}{2}$ cup chocolate chips to banana-bread mixture.

BANANA-RAISIN BREAD PUDDING

Substitute cinnamon-raisin bread for white bread.

LEMON MOUSSE

You can serve this mousse by itself or top it with a drizzle of a berry sauce for color and taste contrast. It is perfect for parties, because you can make it early in the day and keep it refrigerated until you are ready to serve.

½ cup cold water
2 envelopes unflavored gelatin
6 egg yolks
1½ cups sugar, divided
½ tsp. salt

1 cup fresh lemon juice
2 tbs. grated lemon zest
4 egg whites
2 cups heavy cream
Raspberry Sauce, page 147, optional

Place water in a small bowl and sprinkle with gelatin. Let stand for a few minutes to soften. In another bowl, lightly beat egg yolks. Stir in ¾ cup of the sugar and salt. Add gelatin mixture and stir until mixed. Transfer egg yolk mixture to the top of a double boiler. Cook mixture over simmering water, stirring constantly with a metal spoon, until mixture thickens and coats the back of spoon. Cool mixture for 10 minutes. Stir in lemon juice and zest. Refrigerate for 10 minutes or until custard just starts to set.

In a large bowl, whip egg whites until soft peaks form. Add remaining 3/4 cup sugar and whip until mixture forms stiff, glossy peaks. Fold egg whites into lemon custard mixture. In a large bowl, whip cream until soft peaks form. Fold whipped cream into lemon custard mixture. Transfer mousse to individual ramekins or a large serving bowl. Refrigerate mousse for at least 3 hours. Serve with *Raspberry Sauce,* page 147, if desired.

ORANGE MOUSSE

Substitute freshly squeezed orange juice for the lemon juice and grated orange zest for the lemon zest.

BLOOD ORANGE MOUSSE

Substitute freshly squeezed blood orange juice for the lemon juice and grated blood orange zest for the lemon zest.

LIME MOUSSE

Substitute freshly squeezed lime juice for the lemon juice and grated lime zest for the lemon zest.

CITRUS MOUSSE

Reduce lemon juice to $1/4$ cup. Add $1/4$ cup freshly squeezed orange juice, $1/4$ cup freshly squeezed lime juice and $1/4$ cup freshly squeezed grapefruit juice. Substitute grated fresh orange zest for the lemon zest.

PEAR CLAFOUTI

Clafouti is a dessert that originated in southern France. It combines fresh fruit and a custard, which is poured on top. Sprinkle the clafouti with confectioners' sugar before serving, if desired.

2 cups peeled sliced pears
1/2 tsp. ground nutmeg
1/4 cup plus 3 tbs. sugar, divided
1/2 cup milk

1/2 cup half and half
3 eggs
1/2 cup flour
1 tsp. vanilla extract

Heat oven to 350°. Spray the bottom and sides of an 8- or 9-inch pie pan with nonstick cooking spray. In a small bowl, toss together pears, nutmeg and 3 tbs. of the sugar. Pour into pie pan. In a blender container, combine remaining 1/4 cup sugar, milk, half and half, eggs, flour and vanilla. Pulse on high until smooth. Pour over pears in pan. Bake 35 to 40 minutes until top is light golden brown and puffy. Cool for 5 minutes before serving.

PEAR-BLUEBERRY OR -RASPBERRY CLAFOUTI

Add 1 cup fresh or thawed frozen blueberries or raspberries with the pears. Omit nutmeg.

PEACH CLAFOUTI

Substitute peeled fresh peaches for the pears and cinnamon for the nutmeg.

CLASSIC CRÈME BRULÉE

Servings: 8

Crème Brulée is a rich, comforting dessert. Adding blackberries provides a tart contrast to the sweet and creamy custard.

3 cups heavy cream
5 egg yolks
1 egg

⅓ cup granulated sugar
1 tsp. vanilla extract
⅓ cup brown sugar, packed

In a large saucepan, beat together cream, egg yolks, egg and granulated sugar. Cook over medium heat, stirring constantly, for about 20 minutes, taking care that it does not boil. Mixture should be very thick. Remove mixture from heat. Stir in vanilla. Pour custard mixture into 8 shallow ramekins, dividing mixture evenly. Cover ramekins with plastic wrap and refrigerate for at least 6 hours, until well chilled. Heat broiler. Sift brown sugar over tops custards to form an even layer. Broil 4 to 6 inches from heat source for 3 to 5 minutes, until sugar melts and bubbles slightly. Serve immediately or refrigerate until ready to serve.

BLACKBERRY CRÈME BRULÉE
Place a few fresh blackberries in each ramekin before adding the custard.

COFFEE CRÈME BRULÉE
Add 2 tbs. instant coffee with the vanilla, stirring until coffee is dissolved.

GLAZED PEARS WITH CARDAMOM CREAM

Servings: 4

This makes an excellent autumn dessert when fresh pears are available. It's very easy to prepare and makes a beautiful presentation.

1 cup heavy cream
3 tbs. confectioners' sugar
1/2 tsp. ground cardamom

4 fresh pears
2 tbs. butter
2 tbs. brown sugar, packed

In a medium bowl, beat cream and sugar with a mixer on high speed until stiff peaks form. Add cardamom and mix well. Cover and refrigerate while preparing pears. Core pears and slice lengthwise into wedges. Pat dry with paper towels. In a medium skillet, melt butter over medium-high heat. Add pears and cook, stirring occasionally, for about 7 minutes, until juices are released. Sprinkle brown sugar over pears and continue to cook until juices are absorbed and pears are glazed. Take care not to let pears scorch. Top pears with cardamom cream and serve immediately.

GLAZED PEARS WITH CINNAMON OR NUTMEG CREAM
Substitute ground cinnamon or ground nutmeg for the cardamom.

GLAZED PEARS WITH GINGER CREAM
Substitute ground ginger for cardamom.

CAPPUCCINO GELATO

This recipe is for serious coffee lovers. Although it may seem strange to mix espresso grounds and milk together, it is the best way to obtain a strong coffee flavor. Raw eggs can cause salmonella; use Egg Beaters instead if you're concerned.

2 cups milk
3/4 cup ground regular or decaffeinated
   espresso beans

3 egg yolks, or 1/2 cup Egg Beaters
1/2 cup sugar
1 cup heavy cream

In a saucepan, combine milk and ground coffee. Cook over high heat, stirring frequently, and bring just to a boil. Line a strainer or colander with a paper coffee filter and suspend over a large bowl. Pour milk mixture into filter and strain; discard filter and grounds. While milk is filtering, combine egg yolks and sugar in a medium bowl. With a mixer, beat on high speed until egg yolks are light yellow in color. Reduce mixer speed to medium and slowly pour hot milk mixture into egg yolks. Cover and refrigerate for at least 4 hours, until very cold. Stir cream into gelato base and transfer to an ice cream maker. Freeze according to manufacturer's directions. Serve gelato immediately or transfer to a covered container and freeze until ready to serve.

FLAVORED COFFEE GELATO

Substitute cinnamon or another flavor coffee beans for the espresso beans.

FRESH RASPBERRY SORBET

Serve a scoop of this sorbet next to a scoop of gelato or other rich vanilla ice cream. You will love the flavor and color contrast.

1 cup sugar

3/4 cup water

1/4 tsp. grated fresh orange zest

4 cups fresh raspberries

In a small saucepan, combine sugar and water and bring to a boil over high heat. Mixture will become clear and syrupy. Place orange zest and raspberries in a large heatproof bowl. Pour boiling sugar syrup over berries and stir to mix. Cover bowl and refrigerate until cold. Pour raspberry mixture into a blender container and pulse until mixture is smooth. Strain raspberry mixture through a sieve, pressing to extract as much pulp and juice as possible. Discard seeds left in sieve. Transfer raspberry mixture to an ice cream maker. Freeze according to manufacturer's directions. Serve sorbet immediately or transfer to a covered container and freeze until ready to serve.

FRESH BLACKBERRY SORBET

Substitute blackberries for the raspberries.

FRESH STRAWBERRY AND GRAND MARNIER SORBET

Substitute sliced strawberries for the raspberries. Add 2 tbs. Grand Marnier just before removing sorbet from ice cream maker.

RASPBERRY SAUCE

Berry sauces are simple to make and can top everything from bowls of ice cream to slices of cake and wedges of pie.

2 cups fresh or frozen raspberries
1/2 cup sugar

In a medium saucepan, combine raspberries and sugar. Cook over medium-high heat until berries burst and sugar has dissolved.

If you desire a smooth sauce, puree fruit mixture with a blender. Transfer sauce to a bowl, cover and refrigerate until well chilled.

BLACKBERRY SAUCE

Substitute fresh or frozen blackberries for the raspberries.

STRAWBERRY SAUCE

Substitute sliced fresh or frozen strawberries for the raspberries.

INDEX

152   INDEX

Serve Creative, Easy, Nutritious Meals with nitty gritty® Cookbooks

100 Dynamite Desserts
The 9 x 13 Pan Cookbook
The Barbecue Cookbook
Beer and Good Food
Best Bagels are Made at Home
Best Pizza is Made at Home
Big Book of Bread Machine Recipes
Big Book of Kitchen Appliance Recipes
Big Book of Snacks & Appetizers
Blender Drinks
Bread Baking
Bread Machine Cookbook
Bread Machine Cookbook II
Bread Machine Cookbook III
Bread Machine Cookbook V
Bread Machine Cookbook VI
The Little Burger Bible
Cappuccino/Espresso
Casseroles
The Coffee and Tea Cookbook
Convection Oven Cookery
The Cook-Ahead Cookbook
Cooking for 1 or 2

Cooking in Clay
Cooking on the Indoor Grill
Cooking in Porcelain
Cooking with Chile Peppers
Cooking with Grains
Cooking with Your Kids
New Recipes for your Deep Fryer
The Dehydrator Cookbook
Edible Pockets for Every Meal
Entrees from Your Bread Machine
Extra-Special Crockery Pot Recipes
Fabulous Fiber Cookery
Fondue and Hot Dips
Fresh Vegetables
From Freezer, 'Fridge and Pantry
The Garlic Cookbook
Healthy Cooking on the Run
Healthy Snacks for Kids
From Your Ice Cream Maker
The Juicer Book
The Juicer Book II
Lowfat American Favorites
New International Fondue Cookbook

No Salt, No Sugar, No Fat
One-Dish Meals
The Pasta Machine Cookbook
Pinch of Time: Meals in Less than 30
    Minutes
Quick and Easy Low-Carb Recipes
Quick and Easy Pasta Recipes
Quick and Easy Soy and Tofu Recipes
Recipes for the Loaf Pan
Recipes for the Pressure Cooker
Rotisserie Oven Cooking
New Recipes for Your Sandwich Maker
The Sensational Skillet: Sautés and Stir-Fries
Slow Cooking in Crock-Pot,® Slow Cooker,
    Oven and Multi-Cooker
Simple Substitutions Cookbook
Soups and Stews
Tapas Fantasticas
The Toaster Oven Cookbook
Unbeatable Chicken Recipes
The Vegetarian Slow Cooker
New Waffles and Pizzelles
Wraps and Roll-Ups

For a free catalog, call: Bristol Publishing Enterprises.
(800) 346-4889
www.bristolpublishing.com